DICEY AND MORRIS

ON

THE CONFLICT OF LAWS

FIRST SUPPLEMENT
TO THE THIRTEENTH EDITION

Up-to-date to January 2, 2001

UNDER THE GENERAL EDITORSHIP OF

SIR LAWRENCE COLLINS

LL.D., LL.M., F.B.A.

WITH

SPECIALIST EDITORS

LONDON
SWEET & MAXWELL
2001

Published in 2001 by
Sweet & Maxwell Limited
100 Avenue Road,
London NW3 3PF
Computerset by
Interactive Sciences Ltd,
Gloucester
Printed in Great Britain
by MPG Books Ltd, Bodmin, Cornwall

No natural forests were destroyed to make this product;
only farmed timber was used and replanted.

Main work ISBN: 0 421 661 402
Supplement ISBN: 0 421 751 606

GENERAL EDITOR

SIR LAWRENCE COLLINS
LL.D. (Cantab.), LL.M. (Columbia Univ.), F.B.A.
One of Her Majesty's Justices; Honorary Bencher, Inner Temple;
Fellow, Wolfson College, Cambridge; Honorary Fellow,
Downing College, Cambridge;
Visiting Professor, Queen Mary and Westfield College, London;
Member, Institut de droit international

EDITORS

ADRIAN BRIGGS
M.A., B.C.L. (Oxon.)
Of the Middle Temple, Barrister;
Fellow and Tutor in Law, St. Edmund Hall, Oxford

JONATHAN HILL
LL.B. (Birm.), LL.M. (Cantab.)
Professor of Law, University of Bristol

J.D. McCLEAN
C.B.E., Q.C. (Hon.), D.C.L. (Oxon.)
Of Gray's Inn, Barrister;
Dean of the Faculty of Law, University of Sheffield;
Chancellor of the Dioceses of Newcastle and Sheffield

C.G.J. MORSE
M.A., B.C.L. (Oxon.)
Of the Middle Temple, Barrister;
Professor of Law and Head of the School of Law,
King's College London

CONTENTS

Contents

Contents

TABLE OF STATUTES

TABLE OF CASES

xi

Table of Cases

Table of Cases

Table of Cases

Table of Cases

Table of Cases

Table of Cases

Table of Cases

Table of Cases

Decisions of the European Court of Justice are listed below numerically. These decisions are also included in the preceding alphabetical table.

Table of Cases

TABLE OF STATUTORY INSTRUMENTS

TABLE OF CIVIL PROCEDURE RULES

CHAPTER 1

NATURE AND SCOPE OF THE CONFLICT OF LAWS

NOTE 46. See also *Higgs v. Minister of National Security* [2000] 2 A.C. 228 (P.C.).   **1–018**

Section 196 of the Employment Rights Act 1996 has been repealed by section 32(3) of the Employment Relations Act 1999. The consequence is that the territorial scope of the employment legislation will be left to the general law, and it will apply, according to the Government, when there is "some proper connection" with the United Kingdom: H.C. Deb. 1998–1999, vol. 336, col. 31.   **1–046**

See Vischer, *International Encyclopedia of Comparative Law*, Vol. III, Chap. 4 (1999).   **1–074**

Chapter 2

CHARACTERISATION AND THE INCIDENTAL QUESTION

2–001 NOTE 1. Add: Lipstein, *International Encyclopedia of Comparative Law*, Vol. III, Chap. 5 (1999); Mistelis, *Charakteriserungen und Qualifikation im internationalen Privatrecht* (1999).

2–013 Under Spanish law it is provided that civil proceedings, if brought separately during the currency of criminal proceedings about the same matter, have to be stayed pending the conclusion of the criminal proceedings; there is also a general rule (albeit one which is subject to exceptions) that, where conduct gives rise to both criminal and civil liability, if criminal proceedings are not brought, the civil proceedings cannot be brought *ex delicto* under Article 1092 of the Spanish Civil Code, but must be brought under Article 1902. One of the many issues raised in *Grupo Torras S.A. v. Al-Sabah* [1999] C.L.C. 1469 (reversed in part on other grounds, November 2, 2000 (C.A.)) was whether these rules are to be regarded as substantive or procedural. Mance J. decided that they are procedural and, in reaching this conclusion, noted (at p. 1662): "Although this is not conclusive, the basic principles are to be found in the Spanish Procedural Code . . . "

CHAPTER 5

THE EXCLUSION OF FOREIGN LAW

See also *Kuwait Airways Corp. v. Iraqi Airways Co.* [2001] 1 Lloyd's Rep.   **5–005**
161 (C.A.) for a discussion of the decision in *Oppenheimer v. Cattermole*
[1976] A.C. 249.

NOTE 45. Order 11, 1(1) has been replaced by CPR, r. 6.20.   **5–010**

NOTE 58. See also *Kuwait Airways Corp. v. Iraqi Airways Co. (Nos. 4 and 5)*,   **5–013**
supra.

NOTE 7. See also *QRS 1 ApS v. Frandsen* [1999] 1 W.L.R 2169 (C.A.), noted   **5–023**
Briggs (1999) 70 B.Y.I.L. 341, Smart (2000) 116 L.Q.R. 360: a claim by the
liquidator of a Danish company against the shareholder of a company in
respect of the stripping of its assets was held to be an unenforceable revenue
claim; the only creditors were the Danish tax authorities, and the claim was for
the indirect enforcement of revenue laws; the claim was a revenue matter
within the meaning of the 1968 Convention and so excluded from its scope (as
to which see main work, para. 11–015) and the rule that English courts would
not directly or indirectly enforce the revenue laws of another country was not
overridden by the 1968 Convention.

NOTE 25. In *Old North State Brewing Co. v. Newlands Services Inc.* [1999] 4   **5–025**
W.W.R. 573 (B.C.C.A.) a North Carolina judgment for treble damages was
enforced.

In two decisions in British Columbia, United States judgments in civil actions   **5–035**
for disgorgement of the proceeds of fraud in favour of the United States
Securities and Exchange Commission have been enforced: *United States of
America (Securities and Exchange Commission) v. Shull* and *United States
Securities and Exchange Commission v. Cosby*, unreported.

NOTE 60. In *United States v. Levy* (1999) 45 O.R. (3d) 129, the United States
Government was granted a *Mareva* injunction in aid of United States proceed-
ings in connection with the illegal resale of Canadian lottery tickets in the
United States.

The decision in *Kuwait Airways Corp. v. Iraqi Airways Co. (No. 2)* [1999]   **5–038—**
C.L.C. 31 has been affirmed by the Court of Appeal: *Kuwait Airways*   **5–041**
Corp. v. Iraqi Airways Co. [2001] 1 Lloyd's Rep. 161 (C.A.). After a review
of the English and United States authorities on public policy, the act of
state doctrine, and the doctrine of judicial restraint or abstention established in
Buttes Gas and Oil Co. v. Hammer (Nos. 2 and 3) [1982] A.C. 888, the
Court of Appeal said that, first, the *prima facie* rule is that a foreign sovereign
is to be recognised as having absolute authority to act within his own territory.
That rule reflected concepts of both private and public international law as to
territorial sovereignty. The rule is founded primarily on the comity of nations

rather than on concern as to giving offence to the foreign sovereign or as to the absence of judicial standards. Secondly, there is a certain class of sovereign act which calls for restraint on the part of municipal courts, irrespective of whether the foreign sovereign acts within his own territory or outside it. In such cases there is a principle of non-justiciability which is, or leads to, a form of immunity *ratione materiae*. The principle of non-justiciability seeks to distinguish disputes involving sovereign authority which can only be resolved on a state to state level from disputes which can be resolved by judicial means. Thirdly, however, the English court would not recognise the act of a foreign sovereign which was contrary to public policy, *e.g.* in the case of discriminatory breaches of fundamental human rights. English public policy in most cases will be at one with, and will be illuminated by, clearly established principles of international law.

The Iraqi decrees confiscating the Kuwaiti planes in the aftermath of the Iraqi invasion of Kuwait were refused recognition. The resolutions of the Security Council had made it clear to all Member States that they were not to recognise Iraq's attempt to annex Kuwait, and a letter to the court from the Foreign and Commonwealth Office had emphasised the commitment of Her Majesty's Government to its obligations under the Security Council resolutions. There was no judicially unmanageable issue of international or diplomatic sensitivity, and the letter from the Foreign and Commonwealth Office left the court free to apply its own principles to the claim placed before it and which *prima facie* it had a judicial responsibility to determine. The Iraqi decree was a fundamentally exorbitant piece of legislation which purported to dissolve a foreign (Kuwaiti) corporation and to affect assets wherever situate, and it would not be recognised even to the extent it affected property in Iraq. The Iraqi resolution was in breach of clearly established principles of international law, and was contrary to English public policy: the context of war and peace was of fundamental importance to the welfare of mankind; the very serious breaches of international law committed by Iraq led to all but universal condemnation in which the United Kingdom shared, and the United Kingdom had set an example, together with most other nations, on a matter of public policy; the act of state doctrine did not preclude the English court from denying recognition to the Iraqi decree, because the doctrine did not require the recognition of a foreign statute which was contrary to English public policy.

The Court of Appeal did not find it necessary to decide whether the act of state doctrine had any applicability at all when the property had been unlawfully brought by the confiscating state within its territory. But it indicated that a submission to that effect had much to commend it, and expressed doubt whether the act of state doctrine applied in that case, where the aircraft of Kuwait Airways Corp. had been brought unlawfully into Iraq.

5–039   NOTE 85. See also *R. v. Home Secretary, ex p. Johnson* [1999] Q.B. 1174; *R. v. Home Secretary, ex p. Launder (No. 2)* [1998] Q.B. 994; *Azov Shipping Co. v. Baltic Shipping Co.* [1999] 2 Lloyd's Rep. 159; *Skrine & Co. v. Euromoney Publications plc*, *The Times*, November 10, 2000.

5–041   NOTE 97. The decision in *Nuova Safim SpA v. Sakura Bank Ltd.* [1998] C.L.C. 306 has been affirmed by the Court of Appeal: [1999] C.L.C. 1830 (C.A.).

CHAPTER 6

DOMICILE AND RESIDENCE

2. ASCERTAINMENT OF DOMICILE

B. *Domicile of choice*

(1) ACQUISITION

In *Bheekhun v. Williams* [1999] 2 F.L.R. 229 (C.A.), a decision to take British **6–041** rather than Mauritius nationality when the latter country became independent was treated as a "clear pointer" to the acquisition of a domicile of choice in England.

NOTE 56. Add: *In the Marriage of Ferrier-Watson and McElrath* (2000) 26 **6–047** Fam. L.R. 169.

3. RESIDENCE

NOTE 21. See also *Leyvand v. Barasch, The Times*, March 23, 2000 (court **6–121** willing to find ordinary residence in two countries; security for costs context).

NOTE 26. Add: *R. v. Kent County Council, ex p. S.* [2000] 1 F.L.R. 155. **6–122**

See Beaumont and McEleavy, *The Hague Convention on International Child* **6–123** *Abduction* (1999), Chap. 7; Rogerson (2000) 49 I.C.L.Q. 86.

The European Court has held (in the context of Council Regulation 1408/71 **6–124** of June 14, 1971 dealing with social security schemes) that in considering habitual residence, account must be taken of the family situation of the propositus, his reasons for moving, the length and continuity of residence, the possession of stable employment (if that be the case) and his intentions: Case C–90/97 *Swaddling v. Administration Officer* [1999] E.C.R. I–1075.

The House of Lords held, in the context of entitlement to social security benefits, that a person newly arrived from Bangladesh and intending to remain in England did not, without more, acquire an immediate habitual residence in England: to acquire an habitual residence, a person must take up residence in the relevant country and live there for a period which shows that the residence has become habitual: *Nessa v. Chief Adjudication Officer* [1999] 1 W.L.R. 1937 (H.L.). The length of that period is not fixed; it must depend on the circumstances: *ibid.*, citing the dictum of Butler-Sloss L.J. in *Re A.F. (A Minor) (Child Abduction)* [1992] 1 F.C.R. 269, 277 that "a month can be an appreciable period of time".

It has been said that the two concepts of habitual residence and ordinary **6–126** residence share "a common core of meaning" but Lord Slynn reserved the question whether the terms were always synonymous; each might take a shade of meaning from the context in which it was used: *Nessa v. Chief Adjudication Officer* [1999] 1 W.L.R. 1937, 1941 (H.L.).

CHAPTER 7

SUBSTANCE AND PROCEDURE

NOTE 1 and text thereto. Rule 17 was applied and the text was cited with approval in *De Gartori v. Smithwick* [2000] 1 I.L.R.M. 463 (Sup. Ct.). **7R–001—002**

In the context of English proceedings, whether or not a document is privileged is to be determined by English law; the fact that under a foreign law the document is not privileged or that the privilege that existed is deemed to have been waived is irrelevant: *Bourns Inc. v. Raychem Corp.* [1999] C.L.C. 1029 (C.A.). **7–014**

NOTE 16. The principle that priorities are governed by the *lex fori* is equally applicable in cases where all the competing claims are governed by the same (foreign) *lex causae*: *Fournier v. The Ship "Margaret Z"* [1999] 3 N.Z.L.R. 111. **7–032**

NOTE 27. See also *Edmunds v. Simmonds*, *The Times*, November 21, 2000, a case decided under Part III of the Private International Law (Miscellaneous Provisions) Act 1995 in which Garland J. held that heads of damage are matters of substantive law and how damages are quantified under those heads is a procedural matter. See, however, *King v. T. Tunnock Ltd.*, 2000 S.L.T. 744, in which the Court of Session (Inner House) decided that, in the context of a claim for compensation under the Commercial Agents (Council Directive) Regulations (S.I. 1993 No. 3053), which implement Council Directive (EC) 653/86, the principles of French law on which the Directive's compensation system is based, rather than the common law rules governing the quantification of damages, are relevant for determining the level of compensation to which the claimant might be entitled. **7–034**

In *John Pfeiffer Pty Ltd. v. Rogerson* (2000) 172 A.L.R. 625 the plaintiff sued his employer in the Australian Capital Territory (A.C.T.) in relation to injury suffered in an accident at work in New South Wales. In the A.C.T. damages were assessed at A$30,000 plus out of pocket expenses; under the Workers' Compensation Act 1987 (N.S.W.) damages would have been limited to a considerably lesser sum. The Supreme Court of the A.C.T. and the Federal Court of Australia, applying *Stevens v. Head* (1993) 176 C.L.R. 433, held that the N.S.W. provision imposing a limit on the damages recoverable was procedural and, therefore, not applicable in A.C.T. proceedings. The employer appealed to the High Court of Australia. The High Court reconsidered the rule laid down in *Stevens v. Head* (that a statutory rule laying down a limit on damages is procedural in nature) and decided that the N.S.W. provision, which places a cap on damages, is a substantive rule. A majority of the High Court (comprising Gleeson C.J. Gaudron, McHugh, Gummow and Hayne JJ.) went further and indicated (at p. 651) that *all* questions about the amount of **7–038** damages that may be recovered ought to be treated as substantive issues. See further entry at para. 35–005, n. 38 and text, *infra*.

7–041 See also *John Pfeiffer Pty Ltd. v. Rogerson* (2000) 172 A.L.R. 625 in which the High Court of Australia indicated (*obiter*) that, at common law, statutes of limitation are substantive, rather than procedural.

7–044 NOTE 73. Add: Briggs (1998) 69 B.Y.I.L. 352, 355.

NOTE 76. *Connelly v. RTZ Corp. (No. 2)* is now reported at [1999] C.L.C. 533.

CHAPTER 8

INTERNATIONAL LITIGATION: PROTECTIVE MEASURES AND JUDICIAL ASSISTANCE

In *Grupo Mexicano de Desarrollo, S.A. v. Alliance Bond Fund, Inc.*, 119 Sup.   **8–002**
Ct. 1961 (1999) the United States Supreme Court decided, by a majority of
five to four, that United States federal courts had no power to grant an
interlocuory injunction to restrain a defendant from disposing of its assets
pending the determination of an action. The decision turned on the scope of
the jurisdiction conferred by the Judiciary Act of 1789 on federal courts over
"all suits in equity," which in previous decisions had been interpreted as
jurisdiction to administer in equity suits the principles of judicial remedies
which were administered by the Court of Chancery in England at the time of
American independence. The basis of the majority decision was that in 1789
(and until 1975, when the *Mareva* practice was developed) there was a well-
established general rule that judgment establishing a debt was necessary
before a court of equity would interfere with a debtor's use of his property.
The minority considered that such an injunction was consistent with the
principles which had been devised and which were being administered by the
Chancery Court in 1789: the development of the *Mareva* jurisdiction was
based on the traditional power of equity to remedy the abuse of legal process
by defendants and the injustice which would result from defendants making
themselves judgment-proof. See Collins (1999) 115 L.Q.R. 601. It should be
noted that generally under State law the plaintiff will be able to obtain an
attachment of assets within the State pending trial. In this case the plaintiff
was seeking to enjoin the disposal of assets in Mexico, where the defendant
was incorporated and had its principal place of business. The connection of
the case with the United States was that the plaintiffs were suing on bonds
issued by the defendant which were governed by New York law and provided
for the jurisdiction of the New York courts. See also *Credit Agricole Indosuez
v. Rossiyskiy Kredit Bank*, 94 N.Y. 2d 541 (N.Y. Ct. App. 2000), where the
New York Court of Appeals applied the decision of the Supreme Court to hold
that the New York courts did not have jurisdiction to grant what in effect
would have been equivalent to an extra-territorial *Mareva* injunction.

NOTE 1. See also Maher and Rodger (1999) 48 I.C.L.Q. 302; Gerhard, 1999
Rev. suisse de dr. int. et de dr. eur. 97.

NOTE 24. Add: *Re Q's Estate* [1999] 1 Lloyd's Rep. 931.   **8–008**

See the United States practice referred to at para. 8–002, *supra*. For the   **8–010**
Republic of Ireland see *Bennett Entreprises Inc. v. Lipton* [1999] 1 I.L.R.M.
81.

Text at note 61. Order 11, r. 1(1)(*b*) is replaced by CPR, r. 6.20(2).   **8–019**

NOTE 60. *Cf. Rowland v. Gulfpac (No. 1)* [1999] Lloyd's Rep. Bank. 86; *Re
Q's Estate* [1999] 1 Lloyd's Rep. 931.

NOTE 62. See also *Amoco (U.K.) Exploration Co. v. British American Offshore Ltd.* [1999] 2 Lloyd's Rep. 772.

8-021 In *Ryan v. Friction Dynamics Ltd., The Times*, June 14, 2000, Neuberger J. said that where the foreign court with primary jurisdiction has made an order equivalent to a world-wide freezing injunction, that does not prevent the English court granting a freezing order under section 25 of the Civil Jurisdiction and Judgments Act 1982, at least in relation to English assets and/or against defendants resident and domiciled in England. But cogent reasons must be given to justify overlapping freezing orders, because they lead to substantial increased costs, and also to a risk of double jeopardy for defendants and the opportunity for forum-shopping by claimants. Where the English order overlaps with a freezing order of the foreign court, it would be sensible to have some indication as to which is to be the court with the primary role for enforcing the overlapping injunctions, and that court should normally be the foreign court. Where a overlapping order is made under section 25 it should normally track the terms of the order made by the foreign court. See also *State of Brunei Darussalam v. Bolkiah, The Times*, September 5, 2000.

8-043 The European Community Convention on the service in the Member States of judicial and extrajudicial documents in civil or commercial matters never came into force, and was overtaken by the extension of the competence of the European institutions by the Treaty of Amsterdam's establishment of an "area of freedom, security and justice". The draft Convention was converted, with very minor modifications, into Council Regulation 1348/2000 (for text see [2000] O.J. L160) binding on Member States and coming into force on May 31, 2001. Statements in the text about, and references to Articles of the Convention, apply to the Regulation and its Articles.

8-049 Order 11, rr. 5 and 6 have have been replaced by CPR, rr. 6.24 to 6.26.

8-064 A U.S. Court of Appeals has held that assistance can only be given where the evidence is to be used in actual or pending proceedings in the foreign court: in the instant case, the foreign proceedings involved an appeal to the French Cour de Cassation where no new evidence could be tendered, and so assistance was refused: *Euromepa S.A. v. R. Esmerian Inc.*, 154 F. 3d 24 (2d Cir. 1998).

NOTE 93. The reference should be to 28 U.S.C. s. 1782.

8-075 NOTE 46. Discovery may be ordered against third parties in some circumstances in which no such order would be made in the country of the requested court: *Fecht v. Deloitte & Touche* [2000] I.L.Pr. 398 (Ont.).

8-080 NOTE 77. Add: *Leyvand v. Barasch, The Times*, March 23, 2000 (no presumption that security will be ordered unless foreign claimant can discharge onus of proving property here); *Cripps v. Heritage Distribution Corp., The Times*, November 10, 1999 (C.A.) (existence of related but distinct proceedings can properly be taken into account).

8-084 NOTE 2. Add: *Bunzl v. Martin Bunzl International Ltd., The Times*, September 19, 2000.

The Treaty of Rome does not require a Member State to treat all its nationals **8–085**
equally, and so does not prevent security for costs being ordered against a
party ordinarily resident in the Isle of Man in circumstances in which a similar
order would not have been made against an English party: *Greenwich Ltd. v.
National Westminster Bank plc* [1999] 2 Lloyd's Rep. 308.

For the practice in Scotland, see *Rossmeier v. Mounthooly Transport*, 2000 **8–086**
S.L.T. 200.

CHAPTER 9

PROOF OF FOREIGN LAW

9–002   NOTE 4. Add: *Glencore International A.G. v. Metro Trading International Inc.*
[2001] 1 Lloyd's Rep. 284.

9–010   Add after end of paragraph: But a finding upon foreign law made by arbitrators is a finding of fact and cannot form the basis for an appeal on a point of law to an English court pursuant to Arbitration Act 1996, s. 69: *Egmatra v. Marco* [1999] 1 Lloyd's Rep. 862.

9–013   NOTE 44. Add: *Glencore International A.G. v. Metro Trading International Inc., supra.*

9–014   Second paragraph. For an illustration of the relative status of various expert witnesses, see *Glencore International A.G. v. Metro Trading International Inc., supra,* at pp. 299–300. A general employee of a foreign company which was the victim of an alleged crime is not competent to give expert evidence on foreign criminal law: see *R. v. Okolie, The Times,* June 16, 2000 (C.A.).

9–016   Second paragraph. The court is not inhibited from "using its own intelligence as on any other question of evidence" : *Glencore International A.G. v. Metro Trading International Inc., supra* at p. 300, quoting *A/S Tallinna Laevauhisus v. Estonian State Steamship Line* (1947) 80 Ll. L. R. 99, 107 (C.A.).

CHAPTER 10

JURISDICTIONAL IMMUNITIES

State immunity and human rights. In *Holland v. Lampen-Wolfe* [2000] 1   **10–002**
W.L.R. 1573 (H.L.), it was argued that to give the defendant immunity would
deprive the plaintiff of a fundamental right of access to the English court
under Article 6 of the European Convention on Human Rights. The argument
was rejected. The case concerned the immunity of a State, and the immunity
was an attribute of the state itself under international law which all other
States by international law were obliged to respect. In *Waite and Kennedy v.
Germany* (1999) 6 B.H.R.R. 499 the European Court of Human Rights held
that immunity granted by German courts to the European Space Agency, an
international organisation (as to which see Rule 21, main work), did not
deprive the applicants of their right under Article 6(1) of the European
Convention on Human Rights to a fair hearing. The Court held that the rule
of immunity had a legitimate objective, namely the protection of international
organisations against individual governments. A material factor in determining whether granting the organisation immunity from jurisdiction was compatible with the Convention was whether the applicants had available to them
reasonable alternative means to protect their rights under the European Convention. The Convention establishing the European Space Agency had a
disputes mechanism for dealing with claims by staff. It was held that an
international organisation cannot be compelled by the principle of proportion-
ality to submit itself to national litigation in relation to employment conditions
prescribed under national labour law. See also *N.C.F. and A.G. v. Italy* (1995)
111 Int.L.R. 153 (European Commission on Human Rights). There are several
cases pending before the European Court of Human Rights raising the question whether to grant immunity is contrary to Article 6 of the European
Convention, including *McElhinney v. Ireland*, arising out of *McElhinney v.
Williams* [1996] 1 I.L.R.M. 276 and *Al-Adsani v. United Kingdom*, arising out
of *Al-Adsani v. Government of Kuwait*, *The Times*, March 29, 1996; 107 Int.
L. R. 536 (C.A.).

NOTE 1. For recent developments in public international law, see International
Law Commission, *Report of Working Group on Jurisdictional Immunities of
States and their Property*, 1999.

NOTE 25. *Schmidt v. Home Secretary* [1995] 1 I.L.R.M. 301 was affirmed   **10–007**
[1997] 2 I.R. 121 (Sup. Ct.).

Order 11, r. 1(1) is replaced by CPR, r. 6.20.   **10–016**

NOTE 60. Ord. 11, r. 7 is replaced by CPR, r. 6.27.

NOTE 66. Ord. 11, r. 1(1)(*d*)(iv) is replaced by CPR, r. 6.20 (5)(d).

NOTE 68. See CPR 6BPD, para. 5.3.   **10–017**

10–027   See also *United States v. Friedland* (1999) 182 D.L.R. (4th) 614 (Ont. C.A.).

10–030   In *Holland v. Lampen-Wolfe* [2000] 1 W.L.R. 1573 (H.L.) the plaintiff was an American citizen and a professor at an American university which provided courses at a number of United States military bases in Europe. She taught at a military base in England which was operated and maintained by the United States government as part of its functions as a member of NATO. The defendant, who was also a United States citizen, was employed by the United States government as education services officer at the base, and in that capacity sent a memorandum to the programme director listing complaints about the plaintiff's conduct as an instructor. The plaintiff commenced libel proceedings in England against the education services officer. The question of immunity fell to be decided at common law because, by section 16(2) of the State Immunity Act 1978, section 1(1) did not apply to proceedings relating to "anything done by or in relation to the armed forces of a state." It was held that since the provision within a military base of education and training for military personnel was part of a state's sovereign function of maintaining its armed forces, the publication of the memorandum in the course of the defendant's supervision of such provision was an act within the sovereign authority of the United States so as to attract immunity.

10–032   Order 11, r. 1(1) is replaced by CPR, r. 6.20.

Chapter 11

JURISDICTION IN CLAIMS IN PERSONAM

NOTE: THE PROVISIONS OF R.S.C. ORDER 11 CONTAINED IN
SCHEDULE 1 TO THE CIVIL PROCEDURE RULES HAVE BEEN
REPLACED, AND IN SOME CASES AMENDED, BY NEW
PROVISIONS IN PART 6 OF THE RULES. THE PRINCIPAL
REFERENCES HAVE BEEN NOTED AT THE APPROPRIATE
PLACES.

The text of the 1968 Convention is in Civil Jurisdiction and Judgments Act   **11–004**
1982, Sched. 1, as substituted by S.I. 2000 No. 1824.

Generally the rules of the Conventions apply where the defendant is
domiciled in a Contracting State, even if the plaintiff is domiciled in a non-
Contracting State; and as a general rule the place where the plaintiff is
domiciled is not relevant for the purposes of applying the Convention rules on
jurisdiction: Case C–412/98 *Universal General Insurance Co. (UGIC) v.
Group Josi Reinsurance Co. S.A.* [2001] 1 Q.B. 68.

Note 10. The 1996 Accession Convention is now in force for the United   **11–006**
Kingdom: S.I. 2000 No. 1824.

Note 12. The 1996 Accession Convention is now in force as between the
United Kingdom, Austria, Finland and Sweden: S.I. 2000 No. 1824. Poland
has acceded to the Lugano Convention: *ibid.*

The Lugano Convention now applies to Poland: S.I. 2000 No. 1824.   **11–007**

The Council Regulation was adopted on December 22, 2000, and will come   **11–011**
into force on March 1, 2002: 44/2001 (E.C.). The text is in [2001] O.J. L12/1,
January 16, 2001.

In *R. v. Harrow Crown Court, ex p. UNIC Centre S.A.R.L.* [2000] 1 W.L.R.   **11–014**
2112 it was held that proceedings against a French company under the Trade
Marks Act 1994 by the trading standards service for forfeiture of imported
clothes falsely labelled as Levi's jeans were in a civil matter and were not
criminal or administrative. The local authority did not have a duty to bring
forfeiture proceedings, nor did it have any exclusive status in bringing such
proceedings. The relief it obtained enured to the benefit of the private interests
of individuals. Accordingly, the proceedings were predominantly concerned
with private interests. Consequently the 1968 Convention applied.

See *QRS 1 ApS v. Frandsen* [1999] 1 W.L.R. 2169 (C.A.), *ante*, para. 5–023:   **11–015**
the rule that English courts will not directly or indirectly enforce the revenue
laws of another country is not overridden by the 1968 Convention.

Note 41. See also *UBS A.G. v. Omni Holding A.G.* [2000] 1 W.L.R. 916.   **11–021**

15

11–028 NOTE 55. See also *Vale do Rio Doce Navegaçao SA v. Shanghai Bao Steel Ocean Shipping Co. Ltd.* [2000] C.L.C. 1200 (claim for declaration against brokers that their principals are bound by arbitration agreement not within arbitration exception).

11–029 NOTE 58. See also *The Ivan Zagubanski*, November 16, 2000, not yet reported, entry at para. 12–131, *infra*.

11–037 NOTE 76. See also *Andrea Merzario Ltd. v. Internationale Spedition Leitner Gesellschaft GmbH, The Times*, February 27, 2001 (C.A.), disapproving *Frans Maas Logistics (U.K.) Ltd. v. CDR Trucking B.V.* [1999] 2 Lloyd's Rep. 179.

11–045 On the practice see Case C–420/97 *Leathertex Divisione Sintetici SpA v. Bodetex BVBA* [1999] E.C.R. I–6747.

11–051 NOTE 14. Add: Case C–8/98 *Dansommer A/S v. Götz* [2000] E.C.R. I–393.

11–052 NOTE 16. *Agnew v. Länsförsäkringsbolagens A.B.* [1997] 4 All E.R. 937 (C.A.) was affirmed on other aspects [2000] 2 W.L.R. 497 (H.L.).

11–055 NOTE 19. See also *Bank of Credit and Commerce International S.A. v. Al-Kaylani* [1999] I.L.Pr. 278 for disclosure orders on applications to challenge jurisdiction.

11–057 Order 11, r. 1(1) is replaced by CPR, r. 6.20.

11–063 NOTE 51. In *Canada Trust Co. v. Stolzenberg (No. 2)* [2000] 3 W.L.R. 1376 (H.L.) the House of Lords confirmed that the critical date for the determination of domicile is the date of the issue of proceedings. Consequently, where proceedings were issued against a defendant domiciled in England at the date of their issue, other defendants outside the jurisdiction could be added under Article 6 of the Conventions even if by the time the process was served on the additional defendants that person was no longer domiciled in England.

11R–076 NOTE 87. Order 11, r. 1(1) is replaced by CPR, r. 6.20.

11–083 See entry at para. 11R–076.

11–086 See entry at para. 11R–076.

11–090 See entry at para. 11R–076.

11–092 Order 11, r. 1(1)(c) is replaced by CPR, r. 6.20(3).

11–093 See entry at para. 11R–076.

11–096 See now *Saab v. Saudi American Bank* [1999] 1 W.L.R. 1861 (C.A.): for process to be validly served under Companies Act 1985, s. 694A(2), on an oversea company at its London branch it was not necessary that the action should be wholly or even substantially in respect of the business of the London branch, unless the connection between the process and the carrying on of the business of the branch was of so little significance that it should be disregarded.

See *Sea Assets Ltd. v. PT Garuda Indonesia* [2000] 4 All E.R. 371: the method of service under Companies Act 1985, s. 694A is not exclusive and the provision of an alternative method under CPR Part 6 was not *ultra vires*. — **11–098**

See entry at para. 11R–076. — **11–108**

Order 11, r. 1(2)(*b*) is replaced by CPR, r. 6.19(2). — **11–117— 118**

NOTE 14. On substituted service see *Cadogan Properties v. Mount Eden Land Ltd.* [2000] I.L.Pr. 722 (C.A.). On methods of service outside the jurisdiction see CPR, rr. 6.24 to 6.26. — **11–121**

Order 11, r. 1(1) is replaced by CPR, r. 6.20. — **11R–120— 133**

NOTE 13. Add at end: see also *National Justice Compania Naviera S.A. v. Prudential Assurance Co. Ltd. (No. 2)* [2000] 1 W.L.R. 603 (C.A.) (costs order against non-party). CPR, r. 6.20(17) now applies to such claims. — **11R–120**

Order 11, r. 4(2) is replaced by CPR, r. 6.21. Rule 6.21(2A) provides that the court will not give permission unless satisfied that England is the proper place in which to bring the claim. — **11–126**

Order 11, r. 1(1)(*d*)(iii) is replaced by CPR, r. 6.20(5)(c). — **11–131**

Order 11, r. 4(3) is replaced by CPR, r. 6.21(3). — **11–133**

NOTE 47. Order 11, r. 1(1)(*a*) is replaced by CPR, r. 6.20(1). — **11R–134**

Order 11, r. 1(1)(*b*) is replaced by CPR, r. 6.20(2). — **11R–137**

Order 11, r. 8A is replaced by CPR, r. 6.20(4). — **11–141**
NOTE 64. See now CPR, rr. 6.19(1) and 6.20(2).

Order 11, r. 1(1)(*c*) is replaced by CPR, r. 6.20(3) and (3A). — **11–143R**

Order 11, r. 1(2)(*b*) is replaced by CPR, r. 6.19(2). — **11–146**

Order 11, r. 1(1)(4)(*d*) is replaced by CPR, r. 6.21(2). — **11–147**
NOTE 81. See also *The Flecha* [1999] 1 Lloyd's Rep. 612.

Order 11, r. 4(3) is replaced by CPR, r. 6.21(3). — **11–149**

Order 11, r. 1(1)(*d*)(i), (ii), (iii), (iv) are replaced by CPR, r. 6.20(5)(a), (b), (c), (d). — **11R–152**

CPR, r. 6.20(7) provides for service out of the jurisdiction if "a claim is made for a declaration that no contract exists where, if the contract were found to exist, it would comply with the conditions set out in paragraph (5)." — **11–154**

Order 11, r. 1(1)(*e*) is replaced by CPR, r. 6.20(6), which provides that the court may give permission to serve out if "a claim is made in respect of a breach of contract committed within the jurisdiction." — **11R–169**

11R–183–   Order 11, r. 1(1)(*f*) is replaced by CPR, r. 6.20(8).
    186

11–189   In *Berezovsky v. Michaels* [2000] 1 W.L.R. 1004 (H.L.) (noted Harris (2000) 116 L.Q.R. 562) an influential American business magazine called "Forbes" published an article alleging that the first plaintiff, a Russian businessman, was a leader of organised crime and corruption in Russia, and that the second plaintiff, another Russian businessman, was his criminal associate. Sales of the issue of the magazine were 785,000 in the United States and Canada, 1,900 in England, and 13 in Russia. Each of the plaintiffs was a frequent visitor to England, and each sought leave to serve English proceedings against the editors and publishers in the United States. It was held that the publication in England of an internationally disseminated libel was a separate tort so as to permit the bringing of an action in England. The burden was on the plaintiffs to prove that England was clearly the appropriate forum, but regard was to be had to the principle that the jurisdiction in which a tort was committed was prima facie the natural forum for the dispute. See also *Chadha v. Dow Jones & Co.* [1999] I.L.Pr. 829 (C.A.).

11R–193–   The provisions of Order 11 dealt with in these clauses have been replaced and
  11–198   simplified by the new CPR, r. 6.20(10), which provides for service out of the jurisdiction if "the whole subject matter of a claim relates to property located within the jurisdiction."

11R–199   Order 11, r. 1(1)(*j*) is replaced by CPR, r. 6.20(11) which provides for service outside the jurisdiction if a claim is made for any remedy which might be obtained in proceedings to execute the trusts of a written instrument where (a) the trusts ought to be executed according to English law, and (b) the person on whom the claim form is to be served is a trustee of the trusts.

11R–202   Order 11, r. 1(1)(*k*) is replaced by CPR, r. 6.20(12).

11R–203   Order 11, r. 1(1)(*l*) is replaced by CPR, r. 6.20(13), which provides that a probate claim includes a claim for the rectification of a will.

11R–204   Order 11, r. 1(1)(*m*) is replaced by CPR, r. 6.20(9).

11R–207   Order 11, r. 1(1)(*n*) is replaced by CPR, r. 6.20(16).

11R–208–   The provisions of Order 11, r. 1(1) dealt with here and in para. 11R–221 now
    217   come under CPR, r. 6.20(18), which provides for service out of the jurisdiction if the claim is "a claim made under an enactment specified in the relevant practice direction." The enactments mentioned in the text are in 6BPD, para. 5, together with Part II of the Immigration and Asylum Act 1999 and Schedule 2 to the Immigration Act 1971.

11R–218   Order 11, r. 1(1)(*t*) is replaced by CPR, r. 6.20(14) and (15) which apply to (a) a claim made for a remedy against the defendant as constructive trustee where the defendant's alleged liability arises out of acts committed within the jurisdiction, and (b) a claim made for restitution where the defendant's alleged liability arises out of acts committed within the jurisdiction.

11R–221   See entry at paras. 11R–208—217.

Order 11, r. 1(2)(*a*) is replaced by CPR, r. 6.19(1).   **11–225**

NOTE 65. Order 11, r. 8A is replaced by CPR, r. 6.20(4).

NOTE 67. On the effect of non-compliance with the requirement in CPR, r. 6.19(3) to state the grounds for entitlement to serve the claim form out of the jurisdiction, see *Trustor AB v. Barclays Bank plc*, *The Times*, November 22, 2000.

In *Agnew v. Länsförsäkringsbolagens A.B.* [2000] 2 W.L.R. 497 (H.L.) it was   **11–245**
held by a majority (Lords Hope and Millett dissenting) that pre-contractual obligations fell within Article 5(1); that the "obligation in question" could comprise the defendant's obligations to make a fair presentation of the risk, and not misrepresent it and to disclose material facts; that these obligations were to be performed in London, and the court therefore had jurisdiction. *Kleinwort Benson Ltd. v. Glasgow City Council* [1999] 1 A.C. 153 was distinguished on the basis that it related to a case where there was no contract at all.

In Case C–420/97 *Leathertex Divisione Sintetici SpA v. Bodetex BVBA* [1999]   **11–249**
E.C.R. I–6747 there were proceedings in Belgium against an Italian company for arrears of commission and compensation in lieu of notice of termination of an agency contract. The Belgian court held that the obligation to give notice and, in the event of failure to give notice, to pay compensation was to be performed in Belgium, but that the obligation to pay commission was to be performed in Italy under the principle that debts are payable at the residence of the creditor. Accordingly it asked the European Court whether both claims under the two separate obligations (neither of which was accessory to the other) could be brought in Belgium as the place of performance of one of them. The European Court held that a court does not have jurisdiction to hear the whole of an action founded on two obligations of equal rank arising from the same contract when, acording to the conflict rules of the State where that court is situated, one of those obligations is to be performed in that State and the other in another Contracting State.

In *Chailease Finance Corp. v. Credit Agricole Indosuez* [2000] 1 Lloyd's Rep. 348 (C.A.) it was held that London was the place of performance of an obligation of a bank to pay under a letter of credit against documents; the letter of credit was opened by a Swiss branch of the bank, and provided for payment upon receipt of documents at the Swiss branch, payment to be as per the beneficiary's instructions; the documents were rejected and the payment was not made; the claim was based on the contractual right of the benficiary to be paid at the place instructed, namely London; the bank's argument that the obligation in question was to accept conforming documents in Switzerland was rejected. See also *The Sea Maas* [1999] 2 Lloyd's Rep. 281; *AIG Europe (UK) Ltd. v. The Ethniki* [2000] 1 All E.R. 566 (C.A.); *Barry v. Bradshaw* [2000] I.L.Pr. 706 (C.A.).

In Case C–440/97 *GIE Groupe Concorde v. The Master of the Vessel "Suhadi-*   **11–250**
warno Panjan" [1999] E.C.R. I–6307 the European Court, not following the opinion of Ruiz-Jarabo Colomer A.-G., has re-affirmed that the place of performance of the obligation is to be determined in accordance with the law governing the obligation in question according to the conflict of laws rules of the court seised. The Court recognised that it had adopted a different approach

in the case of contracts of employment, where it had ruled that the place of performance should be determined by reference to uniform criteria, which led to the choice of the place where the employee actually performed the work covered by the contract: Case C–125/92 *Mulox IBC v. Geels* [1993] E.C.R. I–4075. But that depended on the peculiar characteristics of the contract of employment, which had been reflected in the 1989 Accession Convention. The principle of legal certainty was one of the objectives of the 1968 Convention, and that principle required that the jurisdictional rules which derogated from the basic principle of domicile should be interpreted in such a way as to enable a normally well-informed defendant reasonably to foresee before which courts, other than those of the State in which he was domiciled, he may be sued. The Rome Convention had standardised the relevant conflict rules. Accordingly it was not appropriate to adopt the formula suggested by the French Cour de Cassation that the place of performance of the obligation should be determined by seeking to establish, in the light of the relationship creating the obligation and the circumstances of the case, the place where performance actually took place or should have taken place, without reference to the law governing the obligation. See also Case C–420/97 *Leathertex Divisione Sintetici SpA v. Bodetex BVBA* [1999] E.C.R. I–6747.

A Belgian court has referred to the European Court the question whether a defendant who has assumed a negative obligation (in that case to act exclusively with the plaintiff in tendering for projects in Cameroon) which is to be performed in every country in the world can be sued in every Contracting State: Case C–256/00 *S.A. Besix N.V. v. WABAG* (pending).

NOTE 39. Add: *Bio-Medical Research Ltd. v. Delatex S.A.* [2000] I.L.Pr. 23 (Irish High Ct.).

11–251 NOTE 44. See *Viskase Ltd. v. Paul Kiefel GmbH* [1999] 1 W.L.R. 1305 (C.A.); *MBM Fabri-Clad Ltd. v. Eisen und Huttenwerke Thale AG* [2000] I.L.Pr. 505 (C.A.); *Ferguson Shipbuilders Ltd. v. Voith Hydro GmbH & Co. AG*, 2000 S.L.T. 229; *Eddie v. Alpa Srl*, 2000 S.L.T. 1062.

11–252 Add: *Montagu Evans v. Young*, 2000 S.L.T. 1083.

11–256 Council Regulation 44/2001 (EC), para. 11–011, *supra*, provides that where an employee enters into an individual contract of employment with an employer who is not domiciled in a Member State but has a branch, agency or other establishment in one of the Member States, the employer shall, in disputes arising out of the operations of the branch, agency or establishment be deemed to be domiciled in that Member State (Art. 18(2)); an employer domiciled in a Member State may be sued in the courts of the Member State where he is domiciled, or in another Member State (a) in the courts for the place where the employee habitually carries out his work or in the courts for the last place where he did so, or (b) if the employee does not or did not habitually carry out his work in any one country, in the courts for the place where the business which engaged the employee is or was situated (Art. 19); an employer may bring proceedings only in the courts of the Member State in which the employee is domiciled (Art. 20(1)).

11–257 The Council Regulation has been adopted and will come into force in 2002. See entry at para. 11–011.

NOTE 73. See also *Compagnie Commercial André SA v. Artibell Shipping Co.* **11–260**
Ltd., 1999 S.L.T. 1051.

NOTE 76. Order 11, r. 1(1)(*f*) is replaced by CPR, r. 6.20(8). **11–261**

NOTE 82. *Murray v. Times Newspapers Ltd.* [1995] 3 I.R. 244 was reversed **11–263**
[1997] 3 I.R. 97 (Sup. Ct.). Add: *Hunter v. Gerald Duckworth & Co.* [2000]
I.L.Pr. 229 (Irish High Ct.).

NOTE 84. See also *Casey v. Ingersoll-Rand Sales Co. Ltd.* [1997] 2 I.R. **11–264**
115.

NOTE 85. See entry at para. 11–011, *ante.* **11–265**

See *Canada Trust Co. v Stolzenberg (No. 2)* [2000] 3 W.L.R. 1376 (H.L.), **11–287**
ante, para. 11–063: the critical date for the determination of the domicile of
the defendant domiciled in England is the date of the issue of proceedings
against him, and other defendants can be added under this clause even if he
subsequently becomes domiciled outside England. It is not necessary for there
to be prior service on the defendant domiciled in England. See also *Zair v.
Eastern Health and Social Services Board* [1999] I.L.Pr. 823 (C.A.); *MacDo-
nald v. Fedération International de Football Association*, 1999 S.L.T. 1129.

NOTE 26. See also *Compagnie Commercial André SA v. Artibell Shipping Co.*
Ltd., 1999 S.L.T. 1051.

In *National Justice Compania Naviera S.A. v. Prudential Assurance Co. Ltd.* **11–291**
(No. 2) [2000] 1 W.L.R. 603 (C.A.) it was held that a non-party to litigation
domiciled in a Convention country could be made liable for costs under the
Supreme Court Act 1981, s. 51, either on the basis that the application did not
involve "suing" him within Article 2, or if it did, that he was being sued as
a third party under Article 6(2).

NOTE 34. See also *Caltex Trading Pte Ltd. v. Metro Trading International Inc.*
[1999] 2 Lloyd's Rep. 724.

In Case C–412/98 *Universal General Insurance Co. (UGIC) v. Group Josi* **11–302**
Reinsurance Co. S.A. [2001] 1 Q.B. 68 the European Court held that reinsurance contracts were not covered by Articles 7 to 12a of the 1968 Convention.
The object of those provisions was to protect the weaker party to a contract of
insurance. The rules protecting a party deemed to be economically weaker and
less experienced in legal matters should not be extended to persons for whom
that protection was not justified. No particular protection was justified in the
relationship between a reinsured and reinsurer, since both parties were pro-
fessionals in the insurance sector. The House of Lords had come to the same
conclusion in *Agnew v. Länsförsäkringsbolagens A.B.* [2000] 2 W.L.R. 497
(H.L.).

NOTE 32. *Papamicalaou v. Thielen* is now reported [1998] 2 I.R. 42. See also **11–332**
Grupo Torras S.A. v. Al-Sabah [1999] C.L.C. 1473, 1532, revd. in part on
other grounds [2001] C.L.C. 221 (C.A.).

NOTE 30. See entry at para. 11–011, *supra.* **11–333**

NOTE 65. See also *Caltex Trading Pte Ltd. v. Metro Trading International Inc.* **11–348**
[1999] 2 Lloyd's Rep. 724.

CHAPTER 12

FORUM NON CONVENIENS, LIS ALIBI PENDENS, ANTI-SUIT INJUNCTIONS AND JURISDICTION AGREEMENTS

12R–001 NOTE 1. Add, as a leading authority, *Lubbe v. Cape plc* [2000] 1 W.L.R. 1545 (H.L.).

12R–002 NOTE 2. Add: *Lubbe v. Cape plc* [2000] 1 W.L.R. 1545 (H.L.).

12–006 NOTE 19. Add: *Sepracor v. Hoechst Marion Roussel Ltd.*, *The Times*, March 1, 1999 (no stay of proceedings where action brought in a court which had jurisdiction under the European Patent Convention and in which the claimant was therefore entitled to proceed).

NOTE 19. Add new paragraph at end: The court has power to grant a stay of proceedings to allow a case to await the outcome of the arbitration of a related claim in a case, which will be exceptional, where such an order is required for the purposes of proper case management: *Reichhold Norway A.S.A. v. Goldman Sachs International* [2000] 1 W.L.R. 173 (C.A.).

12–007 Order 11, r. 1(1) has been replaced by CPR, r. 6.20.

12–012 NOTE 45. *Cf. Lough Neagh Exploration Co. v. Morrice* [1999] N.I. 258.

12–015 NOTE 52. *Turner v. Grovit* is now reported at [2000] Q.B. 345 (C.A.), and is under appeal to the House of Lords.

12–016 NOTES 54, 58. *Haji-Ioannou v. Frangos* [1999] 2 Lloyd's Rep. 337 (C.A.) is noted by Briggs (1999) 70 B.Y.I.L. 326.

12–017 NOTE 60. Insert, after *Re Polly Peck International plc (No. 2)* [1998] 3 All E.R. 812 (C.A.): *Mercury Telecommunications Ltd. v Communications Telesystems International* [1999] 2 All E.R. (Comm.) 33; *Eli Lilly & Co. v. Novo Nordisk A/S* [2000] I.L.Pr. 73 (C.A.); *Ace Insurance S.A.-N.V. v. Zurich Insurance Co.* [2000] 2 Lloyd's Rep. 418 (right to obtain a stay is not limited to an English-domiciled defendant).

For the position in Ireland, see *Intermetal Group Ltd. v. Worslade Trading Ltd.* [1998] 12 I.R. 1.

12–018 Add at end of paragraph. In *Lubbe v. Cape plc* [2000] 1 W.L.R. 1545, 1561–62 (H.L.) Lord Bingham of Cornhill stated that had it otherwise been shown to be appropriate to stay the proceedings brought against Cape plc, which was domiciled in England, in favour of the courts of South Africa, he would have made a reference to the European Court for a ruling on the applicability of Article 2, as the answer to the question raised and decided in *Re Harrods (Buenos Aires) Ltd.* [1992] Ch. 72 (C.A.) was not clear.

NOTE 68. In Case C–387/98 *Coreck Maritime GmbH v. Handelsveem B.V.,*   **12–019**
The Times, December 1, 2000 it was said that where a court was seised of a
case in which there was an agreement conferring jurisdiction on the courts of
a non-Contracting State, it should assess its validity by reference to its own
conflict of laws.

Order 11, r. 1(1) is replaced by CPR, r. 6.20.   **12–020**

NOTE 76. Add: *Merrill Lynch v. Raffa, The Times,* June 14, 2000.   **12–021**

Text to note 86. In *Lubbe v. Cape plc* [2000] 1 W.L.R. 1545 (H.L.) the House   **12–023**
of Lords upheld the decision of the Court of Appeal at [1999] I.L.Pr. 113
(C.A.) and refused to stay the action. But it disapproved the proposition that
because the South African court had jurisdiction only by reason of an undertaking by the defendant to submit to its jurisdiction, it was not an "available"
forum in the sense of the first limb of the *Spiliada* test: see at pp. 1556 (Lord
Bingham of Cornhill), 1562–66 (Lord Hope of Craighead). It is sufficient that
the undertaking to submit has been given by the time of the hearing of the
application for a stay.

NOTE 89. Add: *Lubbe v. Cape plc* [2000] 1 W.L.R. 1545 (H.L.).

Add after text to note 94: In the case of an international libel, the court should   **12–024**
confine its attention to publication only in the country or countries pleaded in
making its assessment of where the natural forum is: *Berezovsky v Michaels*
[2000] 1 W.L.R. 1004 (H.L.) (noted Harris (2000) 116 L.Q.R. 562) (a case on
service out of the jurisdiction); see also *Chadha v. Dow Jones & Co. Inc.*
[1999] I.L.Pr. 829 (C.A.).

Add at end: Even if the English court has been given jurisdiction by means
of a valid and binding choice of court agreement, the proceedings may still be
stayed on *forum non conveniens* grounds, though strong reason will be
required for such an order to be granted, and the existence of the jurisdiction
clause does not oust the power of the court to stay the proceedings: *U.B.S.*
A.G. v. Omni Holding A.G. [2000] 1 W.L.R. 916.

NOTE 99. Order 11, r. 1(1) is replaced by CPR r. 6.20.   **12–025**

NOTE 2. The English court may take account of the inexperience of the foreign
judiciary in the handling of group litigation in assessing the overall argument
that it would be unjust to order a stay: *Lubbe v. Cape plc* [2000] 1 W.L.R.
1545, 1560 (H.L.).

See also *Radhakrishna Hospitality Service Pte. Ltd. v. E.I.H. Ltd.* [1999] 2
Lloyd's Rep. 249 (delay and lower level of damages not indicative of a lack
of substantial justice); *Mercury Telecommunications Ltd. v. Communications
Telesystems International* [1999] 2 All E.R. (Comm.) 33 (if natural forum is
contractually agreed, a very strong case will be needed to justify the court in
not allowing the case to proceed in it).

Add after second sentence: In *Lubbe v. Cape plc* [2000] 1 W.L.R. 1545 (H.L.)   **12–026**
it was held that the practical impossibility of the claimants' being able to
obtain the funding to commission the requisite expert evidence, and to prosecute the claim before the South African courts, was of substantial weight in
demonstrating that it would be unjust to impose a stay of proceedings. It
followed that as a stay would not be ordered in any case where the claimant

would lack adequate funding and legal representation which he needed in order to obtain justice in the foreign court, Article 6 of the European Convention on Human Rights will not support any conclusion which is not already reached on the application of *Spiliada* principles: *Lubbe*, at p. 1561. *Hewitson v Hewitson* [1999] 2 F.L.R. 74 must be read in the light of the decision in *Lubbe* on this point.

12–027   Add at end: It was stated in *Lubbe v. Cape plc* [2000] 1 W.L.R. 1545, 1561, 1566–67 (H.L.) that no account was to be taken of factors of public interest which were not related to the private interests of the parties and to the ends of justice. It appears to follow that a concern to remove cases from a crowded court list, in the broad interests of those litigants who have a better claim to a quick hearing, is irrelevant (see, for the view that this should be a relevant point, *James Hardie Industries Pty. Ltd. v Grigor* (1998) 45 N.S.W.L.R. 20, 40, 43 (N.S.W. C.A.)).

NOTE 10. Add: *Tiernan v. Magen Insurance Co Ltd* [2000] I.L.Pr. 517 (preference for the conflict rules of the forum—*in casu* those of the Rome Convention).

NOTE 11. Add: *Lubbe v. Cape plc* [2000] 1 W.L.R. 1545, 1560 (H.L.).

12–032   After second sentence, add: If an application for a stay is dismissed, but the defendant proposes to appeal or to seek permission to appeal, he needs to obtain an extension of time for acknowledgment of service, because the original suspension of the time limited will have come to an end with the dismissal of the application for a stay: *Sithole v. Thor Chemicals Holdings Ltd., The Times*, February 5, 1999 (C.A.).

12–033   NOTE 27. See also Widmer and Maurenbrecher, in *International Practice of Law: Liber Amicorum for Thomas Bär and Robert Karrer* (1997), p. 263; Von Mehren, in *Festschrift Drobnig* (ed. Basedow et al. 1999), p. 409.

12–034   Second sentence. The proposition that proceedings for a declaration of non-liability must be viewed with great caution was treated with reservation by the Court of Appeal in *Messier Dowty Ltd. v. Sabena S.A.* [2000] 1 W.L.R. 2040 (C.A.). The court should check that the procedure for obtaining such relief is not invoked abusively, but the declaration may serve a useful function, and it is wrong to circumscribe its utility by artificial limits wrongly related to jurisdiction. And where jurisdiction is conferred over the defendant to the action by the 1968 or Lugano Conventions, there is no basis for making allegations of forum shopping against the claimant.
Order 11, r. 1(1) is replaced by CPR, r. 6.20.

12–035   Add at end: In *Messier Dowty Ltd. v. Sabena S.A.* [2000] 1 W.L.R. 2040 (C.A.) (which was applied in *Chase v. Ram Technical Services Ltd.* [2000] 2 Lloyd's Rep. 418) the Court of Appeal held that the sole test to be applied was whether it would be useful in the circumstances to make the declaration, and "subject to the exercise of appropriate circumspection" there should in such cases be no reluctance to grant such relief.

NOTE 38: Add *Tiernan v. Magen Insurance Co. Ltd.* [2000] I.L.Pr. 517.

12–036   Add at end: Moreover, the proposition that proceedings for a declaration of non-liability must be viewed with great caution was treated with reservation by the Court of Appeal in *Messier Dowty Ltd. v. Sabena S.A.* [2000] 1 W.L.R. 2040 (C.A.). Where jurisdiction is conferred over the defendant to the action by the 1968 or Lugano Conventions, there is no basis for making allegations of forum shopping against the claimant.

Order 11, r. 1(1) is replaced by CPR, r. 6.20. **12–037**

NOTE 51. Order 11, r. 4(3) is replaced by CPR r. 6.21(3).

Text to note 58. In *Lubbe v. Cape plc* [2000] 1 W.L.R. 1545 (H.L.) it was held **12–038** that it would be unjust to stay proceedings under Clause (2) of this Rule where to do so would deprive the claimant of the financial support or legal representation which he required for the bringing of the claim.

NOTE 60. For judicial acceptance of the proposition that a potential claimant **12–039** is therefore wise to start anticipated proceedings without delay, even though this contradicts the underlying policy of the Civil Procedure Rules, see *Messier Dowty Ltd. v. Sabena S.A.* [2000] 1 W.L.R. 2040 (C.A.).

NOTE 62. See also *Andrea Merzario Ltd. v. Internationale Spedition Leitner* **12–040** *Gesellscahft GmbH, The Times*, February 27, 2001 (C.A.), disapproving *Frans Maas Logistics (U.K.) Ltd. v. C.D.R. Trucking B.V.* [1999] 2 Lloyd's Rep. 179.

NOTE 63. Likewise if the essential subject matter of the dispute is arbitration: *The Ivan Zagubanski*, November 16, 2000, not yet reported.

NOTE 74. *Cf. U.B.S. A.G. v. Omni Holding A.G.* [2000] 1 W.L.R. 916 **12–042** (proceedings in another Contracting State, but in a matter falling outside the scope of the Convention).

Add at end of first sentence: It was held in *Glencore International A.G. v. Shell* **12–048** *International Trading and Shipping Co. Ltd.* [1999] 2 Lloyd's Rep. 692 that the court was required to identify the essential issue raised between the parties.

NOTE 98. Add after *The Happy Fellow* [1998] 1 Lloyd's Rep. 13 (C.A.): But it was observed in *Glencore International A.G. v. Shell International Trading and Shipping Co. Ltd.* [1999] 2 Lloyd's Rep. 692 that there was no reason to consider an action to enforce a claim of liability to have the same cause of action as a limitation action. Add at end: *Eli Lilly & Co. v. Novo Nordisk A/S* [2000] I.L.Pr. 73 (C.A.) (actions to rectify contract and to obtain a ruling on the interpretation of the contract not the same cause of action: a case decided at common law and not under Article 21); *Glencore International A.G. v. Metro Trading International* [1999] 2 Lloyd's Rep. 632; *Glencore International A.G. v. Shell International Trading and Shipping Co. Ltd.* [1999] 2 Lloyd's Rep. 692 (claim for substantive relief in relation to property and proceedings for interpleader relief not the same cause of action); *The Winter* [2000] 2 Lloyd's Rep. 298 (possibility of substantive issues being determined by foreign court in interlocutory proceedings leads to application of Article 21).

Add at end of paragraph: In *Molins p.l.c. v G.D. SpA* [2000] 1 W.L.R. 1741 **12–050** (C.A.) it was explained that this meant that the requirements for an action to be definitively pending had to be fulfilled. Accordingly in a case where Italian law required process to be served for the action to become definitively pending, but service had been irregular, the proceedings were not definitively pending unless and until this irregularity was cured by appearance or by order of the judge. In the interim period the court was not seised.

NOTE 4. The new Council Regulation (*ante,* para. 11–011), which will come into effect in March 2002, contains in Article 30 the provisions summarised in the note.

12–051 In *Canada Trust Co. v. Stolzenberg (No. 2)* [2000] 3 W.L.R. 1376 (H.L.), a case concerning the meaning of "sued" in Articles 2 and 6 of the Lugano Convention (see entry at para. 11–063, *ante*), the House of Lords declined to rule on the correctness of *Dresser U.K. Ltd. v. Falcongate Freight Management Ltd.* [1992] Q.B. 502 (C.A.). See also the elaborate discussion by Lord Hoffmann at pp. 1389–1394.

12–053 NOTE 11. Add *Glencore International A.G. v. Metro Trading International Inc.* [1999] 2 Lloyd's Rep. 632.

NOTE 13. *Cf. Molins plc v. G.D. SpA* [2000] 1 W.L.R. 1741 (C.A.), para. 12–050, *supra*.

12–055 First sentence. An action is not pending at first instance if all that remains alive is an appeal against the striking out of the action: *Lough Neagh Exploration Ltd v. Morrice* [1999] N.I. 258 (C.A.).

12–057 See generally Briggs, in *Lex Mercatoria: Essays in Honour of Francis Reynolds* (ed. Rose, 2000), p. 219.

NOTE 26. In line 24, delete the reference for *Allstate Life Insurance Co. v. A.N.Z. Banking Corporation* and substitute (1996) 64 F.C.R. 1, 44, 61 (Aust. Fed. Ct.).

12–058 Text prior to note 34. *Cf. Amoco (U.K.) Exploration Co. v. British American Offshore Ltd.* [1999] 2 Lloyd's Rep. 772.

12–063 NOTE 59. Add at end: *Allstate Life Insurance Co v. A.N.Z. Banking Corp. Ltd.* (1996) 64 F.C.R. 61 (Aust. Fed. Ct.) (application for discovery under U.S.C. s.1782 restrained).

NOTE 62. *Cf. Shell International Petroleum Co. Ltd. v. Coral Oil Co. Ltd.* [1999] 2 Lloyd's Rep. 606 (claim utterly absurd).

NOTE 66. *Cf. Turner v. Grovit* [2000] Q.B. 345 (C.A.) (claim advanced in foreign proceedings could have been brought in English action, even if only as counterclaim: injunction granted).

12–065 Add after third sentence: But *cf. Shell International Petroleum Co. Ltd. v. Coral Oil Co. Ltd.* [1999] 2 Lloyd's Rep. 606 (prior proceedings having been brought in England gave the English court sufficient interest to act, even if it was not *the* natural forum).

NOTE 71. See also *Amoco (U.K.) Exploration Co. v. British American Offshore Ltd.* [1999] 2 Lloyd's Rep. 772.

12–066 Second sentence. In *Turner v. Grovit* [2000] Q.B. 345 (C.A.) (noted Briggs (1999) 70 B.Y.I.L. 332, Harris (1999) 115 L.Q.R. 576, Hartley (2000) 49

I.C.L.Q. 166), under appeal to the House of Lords, it was held that as proceedings had been brought in the courts of a Contracting State which should have concluded that they had no jurisdiction, an injunction would be granted.

NOTE 73. Add: *First Security National Bank Association v. Air Gabon* [1999] I.L.Pr. 617 (usual to apply to second seised court for relief under Article 21 rather than to apply to court first seised for an anti-suit injunction).

See also Briggs, in *Lex Mercatoria: Essays in Honour of Francis Reynolds* (ed. Rose, 2000), p. 219.   **12–069**

NOTE 90. On the effect of delay in application, see the divergent views expressed in *Donohue v. Armco Inc.* [2000] 1 Lloyd's Rep. 579 (C.A.).

NOTE 94. It was said in *Amoco (U.K.) Exploration Co. v. British American Offshore Ltd.* [1999] 2 Lloyd's Rep. 772 that whether an application could or should have been made to the foreign court was relevant to the exercise of the court's discretion.

Illustration 3. Ord. 11, r. 1(1) is replaced by CPR, r. 6.20.   **12–070**

Illustration 4. Ord. 11, r. 1(1) is replaced by CPR r. 6.20.   **12–071**

NOTE 17. The decision in *AIG Europe (U.K.) Ltd. v. The Ethniki* was affirmed   **12–075**
by the Court of Appeal: [2000] 2 All E.R. 566 (C.A.). Accordingly the incorporation of a jurisdiction agreement into one contract from another is a matter for construing the intention of the parties by reference to the law which governs the contract alleged to have effected the incorporation.

NOTE 31. Add at end of first sentence: *Sinochem International Oil (London)*   **12–078**
Co. Ltd. v. Mobil Sales and Supply Corp. [2000] 1 Lloyd's Rep. 670.

NOTE 34. Add: *Mercury Communications Ltd. v. Communications Telesystems*   **12–079**
International [1999] 2 All E.R. (Comm.) 33, where it was suggested that the effect of a non-exclusive jurisdiction agreement was, if anything, stronger than the proposition in the text would suggest.

NOTE 36. Insert before *Sarabia v. The Ocean Mindoro* [1997] 2 W.W.R. 116:   **12–080**
Donohue v. Armco Inc. [2000] 1 Lloyd's Rep. 579 (C.A.) (conspiracy, fraud and Racketeer Influenced and Corrupt Organisations Act (R.I.C.O.) claims within ambit of jurisdiction agreement); *Youell v. Kara Mara Shipping Co. Ltd.* [2000] 2 Lloyd's Rep. 102 (claim in form of direct action by victim against tortfeasor's insurer contractual in nature and therefore subject to jurisdiction agreement in contract of insurance).

Add at end of first sentence: For the case of two contracts, each containing   **12–083**
jurisdiction agreements but which are different or inconsistent, see *Sinochem International Oil (London) Co. Ltd. v. Mobil Sales and Supply Corp.* [2000] 1 Lloyd's Rep. 670.

NOTE 48. Ord. 11 is replaced by CPR, r. 6.20.   **12–085**

NOTE 51. Add at end: *Morrison v. Society of Lloyd's* [2000] I.L.Pr. 92 (N.B.).

12–087 NOTE 58. Add at end: It was suggested in *AIG Europe (U.K.) Ltd v. The Ethniki* [2000] 2 All E.R. 566 (C.A.) that the formal requirements set out in Article 17 may be applicable when it had to be decided whether a jurisdiction agreement in one contract had been incorporated by reference into another.

12–090 NOTE 66. Add Case C–387/98 *Coreck Maritime GmbH v. Handelsveem B.V., The Times*, December 1, 2000, where at para. 19 of the judgment it was stated that a court seised of a case to which a jurisdiction agreement conferring jurisdiction on the courts of a non-Contracting State applies must assess the validity of the clause according to the applicable law, including conflicts rules, thereby confirming the view expressed in the text to this note.

12–093 Third sentence. *Cf. LAFI Office v. Meridien Animal Health* [2000] 2 Lloyd's Rep. 51.

12–096 NOTE 83. Add: *LAFI Office v. Meridien Animal Health* [2000] 2 Lloyd's Rep. 51 (dispute as to incorporation matter for English law to determine); *AIG Europe (UK) Ltd v. The Ethniki* [2000] 2 All E.R. 566 (C.A.) (incorporation of jurisdiction from another document a matter for the applicable law of the contract, but it may be proper to apply Article 17 instead); *Implants International v. Stratec Medical* [1999] 2 All E.R. (Comm.) 933 (agreement not intended to be legally binding is not within Article 17).

12–099 The new Council Regulation (para. 11–011, *supra*) provides that any communication by electronic means which provides a durable record of the agreement shall be equivalent to writing (Art. 23(2)).

12–100 Add after first sentence: In Case C–387/98 *Coreck Maritime GmbH v. Handelsveem B.V., The* Times, December 1, 2000, it was held, following Case 71/83 *The Tilly Russ* [1984] E.C.R. 2417 and Case C–159/97 *Trasporti Castelletti Spedizioni Internazionali S.p.A. v. Hugo Trumpy SpA* [1999] E.C.R. I–1597, that the formal validity of the jurisdiction clause in a bill of lading was to be assessed by reference to the relationship between the parties to the original contract, and not by reference to the written consent or otherwise of a third party said to be bound by the agreement. If under the national law applied by the court seised (in England, the law governing the contract containing the jurisdiction clause) a third party succeeds to rights and obligation of the bill of lading (or other contract), it is irrelevant that he has not separately "accepted" or otherwise indicated his consent to the jurisdiction clause. But if, by contrast, he did not, as a matter of national law, succeed to these rights and obligations, the court must determine by reference to Article 17 whether he did actually accept the jurisdiction clause before it may be relied on against him.

NOTE 91. Case 71/83 *The Tilly Russ* [1984] E.C.R. 2417 was applied in *Glencore International A.G. v. Metro Trading International Inc.* [1999] 2 Lloyd's Rep. 632.

12–103 NOTE 98. See also Case C–387/98 *Coreck Maritime GmbH v. Handelsveem B.V., supra.*

12–106 Add after first sentence: In Case C–387/98 *Coreck Maritime GmbH v. Handelsveem B.V., supra*, it was held that the nomination of the courts "in the country where the carrier has his principal place of business" was sufficient for the purposes of Article 17 as it stated objective factors which expressed the agreement of the parties and which were precise enough to enable the court to ascertain whether it had jurisdiction.

NOTE 6. Add to the list of English authorities: *Mercury Communications Ltd.* **12–107**
v. Communications Telesystems International [1999] 2 All E.R. (Comm.)
33.

Order 11, r. 1(1)(*iv*) is replaced by CPR, r. 6.20(5)(d). **12–111**

NOTE 18: Ord. 11, r. 1(2) is replaced by CPR, r. 6.19.

Order 11, r. 1(1)(*iv*) is replaced by CPR, r. 6.20(5)(d). **12–112**

Text to note 23. Similarly, even if the English court has been given jurisdiction **12–114**
by means of a valid and binding choice of court agreement, the proceedings
may still be stayed on *forum non conveniens* grounds, though strong reason
will be required for such an order to be granted, and the existence of the
jurisdiction clause does not oust the power of the court to stay the proceedings: *U.B.S. A.G. v. Omni Holding A.G.* [2000] 1 W.L.R. 916.

NOTE 31. *Cf. Ingosstrakh Ltd. v. Latvian Shipping Co.* [2000] I.L.Pr. 164 **12–117**
(C.A.) (stay in favour of courts of Latvia).

Add at end of paragraph: *Cf. Baghlaf Al Zafer Factory Co. Br. for Industry v.* **12–119**
Pakistan National Shipping Co. (No. 2) [2000] 1 Lloyd's Rep. 1 (C.A.) (if it
appears that the defendant may not be able to cause the court to overlook the
time bar, it may be inappropriate to order a stay).

NOTE 38: Ord. 11, r. 1(1) is replaced by CPR r. 6.20. **12–120**

Add at end of second sentence: *Youell v. Kara Mara Shipping Co. Ltd.* [2000] **12–123**
2 Lloyd's Rep. 102.

Text to Note 58. Moreover, in *Donohue v. Armco Inc.* [2000] 1 Lloyd's Rep. **12–126**
579 (C.A.) it was considered that the fact that the foreign court had been
applied to and had refused jurisdictional relief was not a sufficient reason not
to grant an injunction.

NOTE 58. Add *Society of Lloyd's v. White* [2000] C.L.C. 961.

NOTE 61. Delete and replace with: *Cf. ante*, para. 12–069. If the decision
whether to order the injunction depends upon whether a foreign statutory
cause of action falls within the scope of the jurisdiction agreement, *Credit
Suisse First Boston (Europe) Ltd. v. M.L.C. (Bermuda) Ltd.* [1999] 1 Lloyd's
Rep. 767 may suggest that the issue should be left for determination by the
foreign court. But in *Donohue v. Armco Inc.* [2000] 1 Lloyd's Rep. 579 (C.A.)
the court construed the agreement in relation to American causes of action,
and ordered an injunction, despite the fact that the American court had refused
to grant corresponding jurisdictional relief.

NOTE 98. Add: *Gilkes v. Venizelos A.N.E.S.A.* [2000] I.L.Pr. 487. **12–127**

NOTE 68. Add: *XL Insurance Ltd. v. Owens Corning* [2000] 2 Lloyd's Rep. **12–128**
500.

12–131 Add at end of paragraph: In *The Ivan Zagubanski*, November 16, 2000, not yet reported, proceedings were brought in London for a declaration that the parties had agreed to arbitrate their dispute, and for an injunction to restrain proceedings, commenced prior to the English action, in the French courts. It was held that, as the essential subject matter of the claim was the validity of the arbitration agreement, the case fell within the arbitration exception to Article 1 of the Convention (not following *The Heidberg* [1994] 2 Lloyd's Rep. 287 on this point), with the result that Article 21 was ineffective to remove the jurisdiction of the English court; and the injunction was granted on the ground that the conflicting views of the French court on the matter furnished no good reason for withholding from a party who had a contractual right to the enforcement of the arbitration agreement.

CHAPTER 13

JURISDICTION IN ADMIRALTY CLAIMS IN REM

NOTE 12. Add: *The Oakwell* [1999] 1 Lloyd's Rep. 249. **13–003**

NOTE 20. In *The Bumbesti* [2000] Q.B. 559, Aikens J. declined to follow *The* **13–004**
St. Anna [1983] 1 W.L.R. 895 and decided that he was bound by the decision
of the Court of Appeal in *The Beldis* [1936] P. 51 (C.A.). Where a dispute
arising out of a charterparty is referred to arbitration, a claim to enforce the
resulting arbitration award is not to be regarded as a "claim arising out of any
agreement relating to . . . the use or hire of a ship" (Supreme Court Act 1981,
s. 20(2)(*h*)).

NOTE 41. For consideration of the 1999 Arrest Convention see Gaskell and **13–009**
Shaw [1999] L.M.C.L.Q. 470.

Second sentence. Section 21(4) of the Supreme Court Act 1981 refers to two **13–016**
points in time: when the cause of action arises and when the claim is brought.
In a case where proceedings are brought in respect of the ship in connection
with which the claim arises, the relevant person must be either the beneficial
owner or a charterer by demise when the claim is brought (s. 21(4)(i)).
However, when the cause of action arises the relevant person may be either
"the owner or charterer of, or in possession or in control of, the ship" (s.
21(4)(b)). In *The Tychy* [1999] 2 Lloyd's Rep. 11 (C.A.) (noted by Baughen
[2000] L.M.C.L.Q. 129; Davenport (2000) 116 L.Q.R. 36) the question arose
as to what exactly "charterer" means in the context of section 21(4)(b).
Although it had been established in *The Span Terza* [1982] 1 Lloyd's Rep. 225
that the term "charterer" includes a "time charterer", the defendant argued
that it did not extend to a "voyage charterer" or a "slot charterer". The Court
of Appeal rejected the defendant's argument; once it is established that a
charterer under a time charter is covered by the term "charterer", it would be
illogical if a charterer under a voyage charter or a slot charter (which is simply
an example of a voyage charter of part of a ship) were not also covered.

NOTE 64. See also *Vostok Shipping Co. Ltd. v. Confederation Ltd.* [2000] 1
N.Z.L.R. 37 (N.Z.C.A.).

NOTE 71. Add: *"Iran Amanat" v. KMP Coastal Oil Pte Limited* (1999) 196 **13–019**
C.L.R. 130 (High Ct. Australia).

CHAPTER 14

FOREIGN JUDGMENTS

NOTE 1. See also Barnett, *Res Judicata, Estoppel, and Foreign Judgments* (2001).

14–025   NOTE 99. Ord. 11, r. 1(1)(*m*) is replaced by C.P.R., r. 6.20(9).

14–027   If the foreign judgment was given in default of appearance, with the result that it is not possible to tell what was the precise basis upon which the judgment creditor succeeded, no estoppel will arise from the individual allegations made in the pleading: *Masters v. Leaver* [2000] I.L.Pr. 387 (C.A.); see also *Baker v. Ian McCall International Ltd.* [2000] C.L.C. 189.

14–029   NOTE 10. On the identity of parties in relation to Article 21 of the 1968 Convention, and its relationship to the principles of *res judicata*, see Handley (2000) 116 L.Q.R. 191, commenting on Case C–351/96 *Drouot Assurances S.A. v. Consolidated Metallurgical Industries* [1998] E.C.R. I–3075.

14–080   Order 11, r. 1(1) is replaced by C.P.R., r. 6.20.

14–081   Order 11, r. 1(1) is replaced by C.P.R., r. 6.20.

14–082   Order 11, r. 1(1) is replaced by C.P.R., r. 6.20.

14–084   NOTE 10. Add at end: See also *Old North State Brewing Co. v. Newlands Services Inc.* [1999] 4 W.W.R. 573 (B.C.C.A.) and *Braintech Inc. v. Kostiuk* (1999) 171 D.L.R. (4th.) 46 (B.C.C.A.), where it was held that American judgments were, in principle, entitled to recognition on the basis of *Morguard*, but (in the latter case) did not meet the standard of a real and substantial connection if the only connection with Texas was the passive posting of material on an internet noticeboard.

14R–127   NOTE 28. Add: *Habib Bank Ltd. v. Ahmed, The Times*, November 2, 2000.

14–129   NOTE 38. Add at end: The resultant state of the Canadian case law was described as "vague" in *Beals v. Saldanha* (1998) 42 O.R. (3d) 127, in that the fraud defence was narrower than in England (and precluded its being advanced when it had been put to and adjudicated on by the foreign court), but it was unclear to what extent it was narrower.

14–145   NOTE 98. To this effect also *Old North State Brewing Co. v. Newlands Services Inc.* [1999] 4 W.W.R. 573 (B.C.C.A.).

14–151   Text to note 18. It was held in *Masters v. Leaver* [2000] I.L.Pr. 387 (C.A.) that where a judgment set out the procedure for obtaining an assessment of quantum of damages, but then did not follow it, that there had been a denial of substantial justice, and one which did not necessarily require to be raised before the foreign court. But in *Minmetals Germany GmbH. v. Fercosteel Ltd.* [1999] C.L.C. 647 (a case on the setting aside of an arbitrators' award) it was held that it was not possible to invoke public policy to point to alleged procedural errors which had already been considered by the supervising court.

Cf. Masters v. Leaver [2000] I.L.Pr. 387 (C.A.).   **14–154**

NOTE 20. In deciding whether the judgment is that of a recognised court, the **14–172** English court is not entitled to go behind the form of the foreign judgment: *Habib Bank Ltd. v. Ahmed, The Times*, November 2, 2000.

NOTE 71. Add at end: Poland became a Contracting State to the Lugano **14R–183** Convention on August 1, 2000: S.I. 2000 No. 1824.

NOTE 85. Case C–267/97 *Coursier v. Fortis Bank S.A.* is now reported at **14–186** [1999] E.C.R. I–2843.

NOTE 10. See entry at para. 14–186, n. 85.   **14–196**

NOTE 31. But *cf.* Case C–7/98 *Krombach v. Bamberski* [2000] E.C.R. I–1935, **14–205** discussed below, where the fact that the court gave judgment without allowing the defendant to be heard was considered to fall within Article 27(1) and Article 27(2) was not mentioned.

Although the content of English public policy is a matter for English law to determine, the outer boundaries of the concept are defined and limited by the terms of Article 27(1), and may therefore be reviewed under the interpretive jurisdiction of the European Court. In Case C–7/98 *Krombach v. Bamberski* [2000] E.C.R. I–1935 and Case C–38/98 *Régie Nationale des Usines Renault S.A. v. Maxicar SpA.*, May 11, 2000, it was held that recognition of a judgment could not conflict with public policy unless this would conflict, to an unacceptable degree, with the legal order of the state in which recognition is sought by reason of the fact that it would infringe a fundamental principle: such an infringement must constitute a manifest breach of a rule of law which is regarded as fundamental within that legal order. In the former case it was held that where the adjudicating court had refused to hear the defendant, on the ground that he placed himself in contempt of court, this could be considered by the recognising court to be a manifest breach of a fundamental right (making the point that where there had been a breach of the European Convention on Human Rights, Article 27(1) of the 1968 Convention may be applied). In the latter case, by contrast, it was held that a mere error in the application of European competition law by the adjudicating court would not constitute a manifest breach of a fundamental right if the remedies available in the adjudicating state were themselves a sufficient guarantee to individuals.

NOTE 33. In Case C–7/98 *Krombach v. Bamberski* [2000] E.C.R. I–1935 it was held that the fact that a court entertaining criminal proceedings, and ordering compensation to be paid to a *partie civile*, had taken jurisdiction over the defendant on the basis of the nationality of the victim of the alleged offence could not be regarded as a basis for withholding recognition on grounds of public policy.

14–206 NOTE 44. Delete first sentence and substitute: In Case C–7/98 *Krombach v. Bamberski* [2000] E.C.R. I–1935 it was held that the fact that a court entertaining criminal proceedings, and ordering compensation to be paid to a *partie civile*, had taken jurisdiction over the defendant on the basis of the nationality of the victim of the alleged offence could not be regarded as a basis for withholding recognition on grounds of public policy.

Add at end: That this is the correct approach to adopt is in effect confirmed by Case C–38/98 *Régie Nationale des Usines Renault S.A. v. Maxicar SpA*, May 11, 2000.

14–209 But *cf. Krombach. v. Bamberski, supra.*, where the fact that the court gave judgment without allowing the defendant to be heard was considered to fall within Article 27(1) and Article 27(2) was not mentioned.

14–215 NOTE 62. The application of this provision when the foreign judgment is not enforceable in the state of origin is the subject of a reference in Case C–88/00 *Italian Leather S.p.A. v. WECO Polstermöbel GmbH & Co.* (pending).

14–219 NOTE 73. For minor amendments to R.S.C. Order 71, see the Practice Direction—Reciprocal Enforcement of Judgments: SCPD 71.

14–220 NOTE 77. *Cf. Citoma Trading Ltd. v. Republic of Brazil* [1999] C.L.C. 1847 (C.A.), where it was held that the measures which may be ordered under Article 39 cease to be valid after the expiry of the period for the bringing of an appeal.

14–224 NOTE 89. Case C–260/97 *Unibank A/S v. Christensen* is now reported at [1999] E.C.R. I–3715.

14–235 First sentence. Delete "Gibraltar, and the Sovereign Base Areas of Akrotiri and Dhekelia" and replace with "any colony": S.I. 1990 No. 2591, Art. 10.

14–247 NOTE 43. Ord. 11, r. 1(2)(*b*) is replaced by C.P.R., r. 6.19(2).

14–248 NOTE 45. But the Canadian legislation, which is limited to anti-trust judgments, is not automatically enforceable, and where it is not made applicable by the Federal Attorney-General, a judgment for treble damages may be enforced in Canada: *Old North State Brewing Co. v. Newlands Services Inc.* [1999] 4 W.W.R. 573 (B.C.C.A.).

CHAPTER 15

JURISDICTION AND ENFORCEMENT OF JUDGMENTS
UNDER MULTILATERAL CONVENTIONS

NOTE 8. See *Andrea Merzario Ltd. v. Internationale Spedition Leitner Gesell-*   **15–003**
schaft GmbH, The Times, February 27, 2001 (C.A.), disapproving *Frans Maas
Logistics (U.K.) Ltd.* v. *CDR Trucking B.V.* [1999] 2 Lloyd's Rep. 179.

Text at note 14. Order 11, r. 1(2)(*b*) is replaced by CPR, r. 6.19(2).   **15–005**

NOTE 32. For the parties to Additional Protocol No. 4 see S.I. 2000 No. 3061.   **15–010**
S. 3(2) of the 1979 Act was brought into force by S.I. 2000 No. 2768.

Text at note 33. See entry at para. 15–005, *supra*.   **15–011**

NOTE 35. Order 11, r. 7 is replaced by CPR, r. 6.27.

NOTE 40. See entry at para. 15–005, *supra*.   **15–012**

NOTE 69. For consideration of Art. 31 of the CMR Convention see *Andrea*   **15–016**
Merzario Ltd. v. *Internationale Spedition Leitner Gesellscahft GmbH, supra,*
entry at para. 15–003, n. 8.

NOTE 73. See entry at para. 15–005, *supra*.   **15–017**

NOTE 75. See entry at para. 15–011, n. 35, *supra*.

NOTE 85. See entry at para. 15–005, *supra*.   **15–019**

NOTE 87. See entry at para. 15–011, n. 35, *supra*.

NOTE 99. See entry at para. 15–005, *supra*.   **15–023**

NOTE 6. See entry at para. 15–005, *supra*.   **15–025**

NOTE 12. See entry at para. 15–005, *supra*.   **15–027**

NOTE 18. Order 71, rr. 40–44 is in Schedule 1 to the Civil Procedure   **15–029**
Rules.

Third sentence. See entry at para. 15–011, n. 35, *supra*.   **15–032**

CHAPTER 16

ARBITRATION AND FOREIGN AWARDS

16–008 When required to determine the seat of arbitration for the purposes of section 3 of the Arbitration Act 1996, the court should have regard not to the whole history of the arbitration leading up to the making of the award, but only to the relevant circumstances up to the point at which the relevant arbitration began: *Dubai Islamic Bank PJSC v. Paymentech Merchant Services Inc.* [2001] 1 Lloyd's Rep 65.

16–010 NOTE 31. See Petrochilos [2000] L.M.C.L.Q. 99.

16–025 The right to appeal from the arbitral tribunal's decision to the court on a point of law (under section 69 of the 1996 Act) arises only in relation to questions of English law. Where the contract between the parties is governed by Swiss law, there is no possibility of an appeal under section 69: *Egmatra A.G. v. Marco Trading Corporation* [1999] 1 Lloyd's Rep. 862. See also *Sanghi Polyesters Ltd. (India) v. The International Investor (KCFC) (Kuwait)* [2000] 1 Lloyd's Rep. 480, where the arbitration agreement provided that the dispute was to be governed by "the Laws of England except to the extent it may conflict with Islamic Shari'a, which shall prevail".

NOTE 84. Add: *Sanghi Polyesters Ltd. (India) v. The International Investor (KCFC) (Kuwait)* [2000] 1 Lloyd's Rep. 480.

16–028 NOTE 91. Order 11, r. 1(1)(*d*) is replaced by CPR, r. 6.20(5).

NOTE 93. The statement that CPD PD49G, para. 8.1 applies only to applications by and against parties to an arbitration and that it does not allow service out of the jurisdiction on a non-party was approved and applied in *Vale do Rio Doce Navegaçao S.A. v. Shanghai Bao Steel Ocean Shipping Co. Ltd.* [2000] 2 Lloyd's Rep. 1.
Text at note 95. Service out of the jurisdiction is effected under CPR, r. 6.20, which replaces Order 11, r. 1(1).

NOTE 96. The relevant part of Order 11 is replaced by CPR, r. 6.20.

16–031 In a case involving an arbitration whose seat is in England, if the parties have chosen the law of another country to govern the merits of the dispute, section 46(1)(a) of the 1996 Act does not impose a mandatory requirement on the arbitral tribunal to obtain general evidence and guidance as to that foreign law; if there is no suggestion by the parties that there is an issue on which the chosen law differs from English law, the tribunal is free to decide the matter on the basis of the presumption that the chosen law is the same as English law: *Hussman (Europe) Ltd. v. Al Ameen Development & Trade Co.* [2000] 2 Lloyd's Rep. 83.

16–038 It is provided that, "[n]o appeal shall lie to the Court of Appeal . . . except as provided by Part I of the Arbitration Act 1996, from any decision of the High

Court under that Part" (Supreme Court Act 1981, s. 18(1)(*g*), as amended). In *Inco Europe Ltd. v. First Choice Distribution* [2000] 1 W.L.R. 586 (H.L.) it was argued that, as the 1996 Act makes no provision for appeals against decisions under section 9, there was no mechanism whereby decisions of the High Court (whether to grant a stay under section 9 or to refuse a stay, such as on the basis that the alleged arbitration agreement is null and void) could be reviewed. The House of Lords held that, in view of the legislative history, the amended section 18(1)(*g*) of the Supreme Court Act 1981 should be read as not excluding appeals from decisions of the High Court under section 9 of the 1996 Act.

NOTE 32. S.I. 1996 No. 3211 is revoked and replaced by S.I. 1999 No. 2167, the effect of which is that, for the purposes of section 91 of the 1996 Act, as long as the other conditions are satisfied, an arbitration agreement is unfair under the Unfair Terms in Consumer Contract Regulations 1999 if it relates to a claim for a pecuniary remedy which does not exceed £5,000.

For the relationship between section 9 of the 1996 Act and section 12 (under which an application for an extension of time in which to commence an arbitration may be brought before the court) see *Grimaldi Compagnia di Navigazione SpA v. Sekihyo Lines Ltd.* [1999] 1 W.L.R. 708.   **16–041**

NOTE 48. *Patel v. Patel* is now reported at [2000] Q.B. 551.

In *Al-Naimi v. Islamic Press Agency Ltd.* [2000] 1 Lloyd's Rep. 522 the Court   **16–042** of Appeal considered a number of procedural aspects of section 9 of the 1996 Act. Before granting a stay under section 9 the court must be satisfied that there is an arbitration clause between the parties and that the subject of the action is within the scope of the clause. Where the court cannot be sure of these matters, the grant of a stay under the court's inherent jurisdiction may nevertheless be the sensible course of action—thereby allowing the arbitral tribunal to determine its jurisdiction under section 30 of the 1996 Act. Although there will be cases in which the court feels unable to resolve the section 9 point without the issue being tried (in which case the court should make an order under CPR PD49G, para. 6.2, which replaced R.S.C. Order 73, r. 6(2)), the court should try to resolve the issue on the affidavit evidence, particularly if the parties agree that they would like the matter resolved on the affidavits.

NOTE 60. See also *Hi-Fert Pty. Ltd. v. Kiukiang Maritime Carriers Inc.* (1996)   **16–044** 150 A.L.R. 54.

NOTE 62. In *Wealands v. CLC Contractors Ltd.* [1999] 2 Lloyd's Rep. 739 the Court of Appeal dismissed the appeal against Tuckey J.'s decision to order a stay under section 9 of the 1996 Act ([1998] C.L.C. 808).

Glencore Grain Ltd. v. Agros Trading Co. [1999] 2 Lloyd's Rep. 410 (noted   **16–047** by Berg [2000] L.M.C.L.Q. 153) raised a question relating to the meaning of "dispute" in the context of an application to enforce an award rendered under G.A.F.T.A. arbitration rules. The contract between the parties provided that where an invoice was not settled without delay "a dispute shall be deemed to have arisen" (clause 11) and that neither party shall bring any legal proceedings "in respect of any such dispute until such dispute shall first have been heard and determined by the arbitrator(s) or a Board of Appeal, as the case may be" (clause 29). It was argued on the defendant's behalf that, as the defendant had admitted liability, there was no dispute between the parties. The Court of Appeal held that "dispute" in clauses 11 and 29 should bear the same meaning and that as clause 11 deemed a dispute to exist in a case of delay in payment, there was a dispute for the purposes of clause 29 (a typical *Scott v. Avery* clause); the fact that the defendant had admitted liability was irrelevant. Although Clarke L.J. left the question open, it is implicit in the Court of Appeal's judgment that, had the case involved an application for a stay under section 9 of the 1996 Act, a stay would have been granted on the basis that the "dispute" deemed by clause 11 was, by virtue of clause 29, a matter which under the agreement was to be referred to arbitration.

NOTE 70. See the entry at para. 16–044, n. 62, *supra*.

16–053 NOTE 89. See Petrochilos [2000] L.M.C.L.Q. 99.

16–055 Where legal proceedings are related to current arbitration proceedings, the court may, under its inherent jurisdiction, grant a stay of the legal proceedings, pending the outcome of the arbitration. In *Reichhold Norway A.S.A. v. Goldman Sachs International* [2000] 1 W.L.R. 173 (C.A.) disputes arose out of the sale of a subsidiary company. J., a Norwegian company, had engaged the defendants as agent to advise and negotiate the sale on terms that the defendants would indemnify J. against consequent liability. The sale agreement between J. and the plaintiffs, which acquired the share capital, provided for disputes arising under the agreement to be referred to arbitration in Norway. The plaintiffs brought an action against the defendants in England, alleging negligent misstatement, and referred disputes under the sale agreement with J. to arbitration. The defendants were granted a stay of the English proceedings, pending determination of the arbitration in Norway.

16–056 NOTE 95. See *Bankers Trust Co. v. P.T. Jakarta International Hotels & Development* [1999] 1 Lloyd's Rep. 910.

16R–058 NOTE 98. *Uniforêt Pâte Port-Cartier Inc. v. Zerotech Technologies Inc.* [1998] 9 W.W.R. 688 (B.C.) suggests that the test for determining whether an award is final and conclusive is the same as that applicable in the context of the recognition and enforcement of foreign judgments (on which see paras. 14R–018 *et seq.* of the main work). The English authorities involving the enforcement of foreign awards have been concerned with awards requiring the payment of a sum of money and there has been no consideration of the enforcement of other types of award. *Uniforêt Pâte Port-Cartier Inc. v. Zerotech Technologies Inc.* indicates that, in the inter-provincial context in Canada, a judgment which confirms an arbitration award is, in principle, enforceable in other provinces notwithstanding the fact that the judgment is not a monetary judgment.

16–062 NOTE 13. *Westacre Investments Inc. v. Jugoimport-SPDR Holding Co. Ltd.* is reported at [2000] 1 Q.B. 288 (C.A.).

16–064 Order 11, r. 1(1)(*m*) is replaced by CPR, r. 6.20(9).

The St. Anna [1983] 1 W.L.R. 895 was not followed in *The Bumbesti* [2000]   **16–065**
Q.B. 559. Aikens J. held that he was bound by *The Beldis* [1936] P. 51 (C.A.)
to conclude that the court does not have jurisdiction under section 20(2)(*h*) of
the Supreme Court Act 1981 in respect of proceedings to enforce an arbitration award.

NOTE 31. Add: *Uniforêt Pâte Port-Cartier Inc. v. Zerotech Technologies Inc.*   **16–068**
[1998] 9 W.W.R. 688 (B.C.).

NOTE 84. See entry at para. 16–062, n. 13, *supra*.   **16–087**

A decision of the Islamic Shari'a Council in London is neither a judgment   **16–109**
(because the Shari'a Council is not a judicial body established under the law
of any State) nor an arbitration award, unless, and to the extent that, the
Shari'a Council's decision deals with matters expressly referred to it by the
parties to a dispute. Where a dispute between parties entitled under a will is
referred to the Shari'a Council by the testator's Trusteeship Council (which is
not a party to the dispute), the resulting decision cannot be regarded as an
arbitration award: *Al Midani v. Al Midani* [1999] 1 Lloyd's Rep. 923.

Second sentence. See *Corporacion Transnacional de Inversiones S.A. de C.V.*   **16–112**
v. STET International SpA (1999) 45 O.R. (3rd) 183, a case concerning an
application to set aside an award under Article 34 of the UNCITRAL Model
Law, which reproduces the grounds for refusing recognition and enforcement
under the New York Convention.

NOTE 50. See also *Irvani v. Irvani* [2000] 1 Lloyd's Rep. 412 (C.A.) which   **16–114**
suggests that there is a breach of section 103(2)(*c*) if it is established either
that the arbitrator's decision was influenced by pressure brought to bear by a
third party or that the award was based on information which was not
available to one of the parties and, therefore, on which that party was unable
to comment.

NOTE 62. See also Freyer (2000) 17(2) J. Int. Arb. 1; Lastenouse, (1999) 16   **16–118**
J. Int. Arb. 25; Petrochilos (1999) 48 I.C.L.Q. 856; Wahl (1999) 16 J.Int. Arb.
131. *Cf. Spier v. Calzaturificio Tecnica*, 71 F. Supp. 2d 279 (S.D.N.Y. 1999)
(application for re-argument dismissed: 77 F. Supp. 2d 405 (S.D.N.Y. 1999))
in which enforcement of an arbitration award made by Italian arbitrators in
Italy and annulled by the Italian courts on the basis that the arbitrators had
exceeded their authority was refused.

NOTE 68. See also *G. v. G.* [2000] 7 W.W.R. 363 (Alta.) in which it was held   **16–122**
that a dispute arising out of a prenuptial agreement which purported to exempt
the parties from the provisions of the Matrimonial Property Act 1980 (Alta.)
was not incapable of settlement by arbitration.
　　Text at notes 71–73. In *Soleimany v. Soleimany* [1999] Q.B. 785 (C.A.) (a
case involving an English award) enforcement of an arbitration award upholding a contract which involved an illicit enterprise, illegal under the law of the
place of performance, was refused on the ground of public policy. By contrast,
in *Westacre Investments Inc. v. Jugoimport-SPDR Holding Co. Ltd.* [2000]
Q.B. 288 (C.A.), it was held that, if an allegation that the underlying contract

was illegal has been raised before the arbitral tribunal and rejected, enforcement of an arbitration award upholding the contract should not be refused on public policy grounds—unless there was fresh evidence which called into question the arbitral tribunal's conclusion on the illegality point. The scope of these decisions was considered by Timothy Walker J. in *Omnium de Traitement et de Valorisation SA v. Hilmarton Ltd.* [1999] 2 Lloyd's Rep. 222 (noted by Hill [2000] L.M.C.L.Q. 311). OTV had appointed H to act as consultant in connection with a public contract in Algeria. Under the terms of the contract, which was expressly governed by Swiss law and provided for the arbitration of disputes in Switzerland, H was entitled to a commission on the public contract being awarded to OTV. OTV secured the contract, but only half the agreed commission was paid. In the arbitration proceedings, OTV argued that H's claim for the unpaid commission should be dismissed on the ground that it was contrary to a mandatory law of Algeria, the place of performance of the contract. The arbitrator accepted that the appointment of H as a consultant "wittingly" breached Algerian law but, because, as no bribery was involved, the contract was not illegal or contrary to public policy under Swiss law, made an award in H's favour. H sought to enforce the award in England under Part III of the 1996 Act and OTV argued that enforcement would be contrary to public policy. Timothy Walker J. held that enforcement of the award would not be contrary to English public policy: OTV's reliance on the *Soleimany* decision was "misplaced" because, in the *Soleimany* case the element of "corruption or illicit practice" was present and "the whole of the judgment of the Court of Appeal has to be read in that context" (at p. 225); the element of corruption or illicit practice was not present in the *OTV* case and, accordingly, there was a parallel with the *Westacre* case, in which the arbitral tribunal had decided that there had been no bribery. However, it should be noted that, whereas performance of the contract in *Westacre* was not contrary to Kuwaiti law, the contract in the *OTV* case involved a breach of Algerian law. Furthermore, the *ratio* of the *Soleimany* case is that, if the English court would not directly enforce the contract because of illegality, it will not enforce an arbitration award based on such a contract; had the dispute in the *OTV* case been litigated in England, the court would have refused to enforce the contract—on the basis of the principle laid down in *Regazzoni v. K.C. Sethia (1944) Ltd.* [1958] A.C. 301 (see Timothy Walker J.'s judgment at p. 224).

For the purposes of Rule 63(5) public policy should be interpreted as including E.C. public policy. In Case C–126/97 *Eco Swiss China Time Ltd. v. Benetton International N.V.* [1999] E.C.R. I–3055 a dispute arising out of a licensing agreement had been referred to arbitration in the Netherlands under Dutch law. The arbitral tribunal ordered the defendant to pay damages to the plaintiff. The defendant applied to the court to have the award set aside on the ground that, because the licensing contract was a nullity under Article 81 E.C. (formerly Article 85), the award was contrary to public policy. During the arbitration proceedings neither the parties nor the arbitrators had raised the point that the licensing contract might be contrary to E.C. law. In response to the questions posed by the Dutch court, the European Court ruled that a national court to which an application is made for annulment of an arbitration award on grounds of public policy must grant that application if it considers that the award in question is in fact contrary to Article 81 E.C. (formerly Article 85). The Court also observed that the provisions of Article 81 E.C. (formerly Article 85) may be regarded as a matter of public policy within the meaning of the New York Convention. Accordingly, in a case where enforcement of an arbitration award is resisted in England on the basis of public policy, if the underlying contract between the parties is contrary to Article 81 E.C. (formerly Article 85) enforcement of the award should be refused.

NOTE 83. See entry at para. 16–062, n. 13, *supra*.   **16–128**

Chapter 17

MARRIAGE

1. FORMAL VALIDITY

17–014   Note 35. Add: Murphy (1996) 47 N.I.L.Q. 35.

2. CAPACITY

17–068   See Murphy (2000) 49 I.C.L.Q. 643. For same-sex marriages, see Bates (1999) 21 Liverpool L.R. 49.

CHAPTER 18

MATRIMONIAL CAUSES

1. DIVORCE, NULLITY AND JUDICIAL SEPARATION

A. *Jurisdiction of the English courts*

The 1998 Convention (as to which see para. 18–013) never came into force, **18R–001** and was overtaken by the extension of the competence of the European institutions by the Treaty of Amsterdam's establishment of an "area of freedom, security and justice". The draft Convention was converted, with modifications, into a Regulation, Council Regulation 1347/2000 of May 29, 2000 on jurisdiction and the recognition and enforcement of judgments in matrimonial matters and in matters of parental responsibility for children of both spouses (for text see [2000] O.J. L160) binding on Member States and coming into force on March 1, 2001. Related changes were made in English law by the European Communities (Matrimonial Jurisdiction and Judgments) Regulations 2001 (S.I. 2001 No. 310). The provisions of the Regulation apply only to legal proceedings instituted after March 1, 2001 (Art. 42(1)). For the present text of the Rule substitute:

English courts have jurisdiction to entertain proceedings for divorce or judicial separation if, but only if,
(a) the spouses are habitually resident in England; or
(b) the spouses were last habitually resident in England, in so far as one of them still resides there; or
(c) the respondent is habitually resident in England; or
(d) in the event of a joint application, either of the spouses is habitually resident in England; or
(e) the applicant is habitually resident in England and resided there for at least a year immediately before the application was made; or
(f) the applicant is habitually resident in England and resided there for at least six months immediately before the application was made and is domiciled in England; or
(g) both spouses are domiciled in England; or
(h) no court of a Member State has jurisdiction under the Council Regulation and either of the parties to the marriage was domiciled in England on the date when the proceedings were begun
Provided that where the respondent spouse (a) is habitually resident in the territory of a Member State of the European Union; or (b) is a national of a Member State other than the United Kingdom or Ireland; or (c) is domiciled in Ireland, the English courts have jurisdiction only under paragraphs (a) to (g) of this Rule.

(Regulation, Arts. 2, 7, 41; Family Law Act 1986, s. 5(2) as amended by European Communities (Matrimonial Jurisdiction and Judgments) Regulations 2001 (S.I. 2001 No. 310), reg. 3(3). Denmark is not a Member State for the purposes of the Regulation: Art. 1(3).).

The Regulation gives jurisdiction to deal with counterclaims (Art. 5) and for a court which has granted a legal separation to have jurisdiction to convert that into a divorce, if the law of that Member State so provides (Art. 6). Article 12 of the Regulation provides that, in urgent cases, the provisions of the Regulation do not prevent the courts of a Member State from taking such provisional, including protective, measures in respect of persons or assets in that State as may be available under the law of that Member State, even if, under the Regulation, the court of another Member State has jurisdiction as to the substance of the matter.

Where the English court is seised of a case over which it has no jurisdiction under the Regulation and over which a court of another Member State has jurisdiction by virtue of the Regulation, it must declare of its own motion that it has no jurisdiction (Art. 9).

Where proceedings are begun in England and the respondent is habitually resident in another Member State and does not enter an appearance, the court must stay the proceedings so long as it is not shown that the respondent has been able to receive the document instituting the proceedings or an equivalent document in sufficient time to enable him to arrange for his defence, or that all necessary steps have been taken to this end (Art. 10(1)); but this provision is replaced by those in Article 19 of Council Regulation 1348/2000 of May 29, 2000 on the service in the Member States of judicial and extrajudicial documents in civil or commercial matters (as to which see para. 8–043) or in Article 15 of the Hague Service Convention of 1965 (as to which see para. 8–040) if the document instituting the proceedings was transmitted abroad under that Regulation or Convention (Art. 10(2)).

For staying of proceedings on other grounds, see para. 18R–227.

18–012   In December 2000, the Government finally abandoned any plans to implement Part II of the Family Law Act 1996.

18–022   Illustration 1. The English court would now have jurisdiction only if W became habitually resident in England and either (a) resided there for at least a year; or (b) resided there for at least six months and acquired a domicile in England: Council Regulation 1447/2000, Arts 2, 7, 41.

Illustration 2. The position is the same under Council Regulation 1447/2000, Arts 2, 7, 41.

Illustration 3. The position is the same under Council Regulation 1447/2000, Arts 2, 5, 7, 41; Art. 5 refers to "counterclaims" which would certainly include H's cross-petition; the position is less clear as to W's supplemental petition.

18R–024   The jurisdictional rules in Council Regulation 1347/2000 of May 29, 2000 on jurisdiction and the recognition and enforcement of judgments in matrimonial matters and in matters of parental responsibility for children of both spouses (as to which see para. 18R–001) govern jurisdiction in proceedings for nullity of marriage (Art. 1(1)(a)). Related changes were made in English law by the European Communities (Matrimonial Jurisdiction and Judgments) Regulations 2001 (S.I. 2001 No. 310). The provisions of the Regulation apply only to legal proceedings instituted after March 1, 2001 (Art. 42(1)). For the present text of the Rule substitute:

English courts have jurisdiction to entertain proceedings for divorce or judicial separation if, but only if,
(a) the spouses are habitually resident in England; or

(b) the spouses were last habitually resident in England, in so far as one of them still resides there; or

(c) the respondent is habitually resident in England; or

(d) in the event of a joint application, either of the spouses is habitually resident in England; or

(e) the applicant is habitually resident in England and resided there for at least a year immediately before the application was made; or

(f) the applicant is habitually resident in England and resided there for at least six months immediately before the application was made and is domiciled in England; or

(g) both spouses are domiciled in England; or

(h) no court of a Member State has jurisdiction under the Council Regulation and either of the parties to the marriage

(i) was domiciled in England on the date when the proceedings were begun; or

(ii) died before that date and either was at death domiciled in England or had been habitually resident in England throughout the period of one year ending with the date of death;

Provided that where the respondent spouse (a) is habitually resident in the territory of a Member State of the European Union; or (b) is a national of a Member State other than the United Kingdom or Ireland; or (c) is domiciled in Ireland, the English courts have jurisdiction only under paragraphs (a) to (g) of this Rule.

(Regulation, Arts. 2, 7, 41; Family Law Act 1986, s. 5(3) as amended by European Communities (Matrimonial Jurisdiction and Judgments) Regulations 2001 (S.I. 2001 No. 310), reg. 3(3). Denmark is not a Member State for the purposes of the Regulation: Art. 1(3).).

Illustration 1. The court now has jurisdiction only after W has become **18–028** habitually resident in England and has resided there for at least six months: Council Regulation 1447/2000, Arts. 2, 7, 41.

B. *Choice of Law*

When it became unlikely that section 9 of the Family Law Act 1996 would be **18–032** brought into force, other approaches to the problem were explored. In *N. v. N. (Jurisdiction: Antenuptial Agreement)* [1999] 2 F.L.R. 745, the wife sought specific performance of an ante-nuptial agreement that obliged the husband to obtain a ghet after a civil divorce. The court held that it had no jurisdiction to enforce such an agreement, but indicated that in appropriate circumstances the grant of a decree absolute to a husband refusing a ghet could be delayed, he could be denied a hearing on ancillary matters, and his refusal might give rise to "financial or other hardship" for the purposes of sections 5 and 10 of the Matrimonial Causes Act 1973. The court cited M. Freeman, *Law, Religion and the State*, in Lowe and Douglas (eds.), *Families Across Frontiers* (1998). In accordance with the approach in *N. v. N.*, a decree absolute was refused in *O. v. O. (Jurisdiction: Jewish Divorce)* [2000] 2 F.L.R. 147.

C. *Recognition of Foreign Decrees*

(2) DECREES OBTAINED OUTSIDE THE BRITISH ISLES

From March 1, 2001 when Council Regulation 1347/2000 of May 29, 2000 on **18R–057** jurisdiction and the recognition and enforcement of judgments in matrimonial matters and in matters of parental responsibility for children of both spouses (for text see [2000] O.J. L160) comes into force, Rules 79 to 82 will apply only in respect of divorces, legal separations or annulments of marriage obtained in countries which are not Member States of the European Union. Denmark is not a Member State for the purposes of the Regulation: Art. 1(3). In relations between Member States, the Regulation takes precedence over the Hague Convention of June 1, 1970 on the Recognition of Divorces and Legal Separations (Art. 37). Insert new material as follows:

(1A) DECREES OBTAINED IN OTHER MEMBER STATES OF THE EUROPEAN UNION

RULE 78A—A divorce, legal separation or annulment of marriage pronounced by a court of a Member State will, subject to Rule 82A, be recognised in England (Council Regulation 1347/2000, Arts. 13(1), 14(1)).

COMMENT

Chapter III of Council Regulation 1347/2000 contains provisions for the recognition and enforcement of judgments pronounced in the courts of other Member States. "Judgment" is defined to include a divorce, legal separation or marriage annulment pronounced by a court of a Member State, whatever the judgment may be called, including a decree, order or decision (Art. 13(1)). Documents which have been formally drawn up or registered as authentic instruments and which are enforceable in a Member State, and settlements which have been approved by a court in the course of proceedings and are enforceable in the Member State in which they were concluded, are subject to the same rules as to recognition and enforcement as judgments (Art. 13(3)). The provisions of the Regulation apply only to legal proceedings instituted, to documents formally drawn up or registered as authentic instruments and to settlements which have been approved by a court in the course of proceedings after March 1, 2001 (Art. 42(1)). With regard to a Member State in which two or more systems of law or sets of rules concerning matters governed by the Regulation apply in different territorial units, (a) any reference to habitual residence in that Member State refers to habitual residence in a territorial unit; (b) any reference to nationality, or in the case of the United Kingdom "domicile", refers to the territorial unit designated by the law of that State; (c) any reference to the authority of a Member State having received an application for divorce or legal separation or for marriage annulment refers to the authority of a territorial unit which has received such an application; and (d) any reference to the rules of the requested Member State refers to the rules of the territorial unit in which jurisdiction, recognition or enforcement is invoked (Art. 41).

No special procedure is required for the recognition of a divorce, legal separation or marriage annulment pronounced by a court of another Member State (Art. 14(1); see also Art. 14(2) on the consequential amendment of records of civil status). Where the recognition of a judgment is raised as an incidental question in a court of a Member State, that court may determine that issue (Art. 14(4)). However, the question of recognition or non-recognition may also be raised by "any interested party" using the procedures prescribed in the Regulation for the enforcement of judgments (Art. 14(3)). Those latter procedures are more appropriately considered below, para. 19–066.

In *Wicken v. Wicken* [1999] Fam. 224, a divorce in Gambia was held "effective" there. Under Gambian law a particular method of proof would be required, but those evidential requirements were matters for the *lex fori* and had no application in England.

18–068

In *Kellman v. Kellman* [2000] 1 F.L.R. 785, it was held in this context but on very unusual facts that "effective" connoted a less rigorous standard than "valid". A "mail-order" divorce in Guam, an incorporated territory of the United States, was *prima facie* not entitled to recognition in any other part of the United States. However, in further proceedings in Guam ten years later, one party attempted to have the decree set aside, but this was refused on estoppel grounds. That judgment was entitled to full faith and credit in other parts of the United States. As a result there was no longer any jurisdiction within the United States in which the validity of the divorce could be challenged, and it was held that in those circumstances, the divorce had to be regarded as "effective".

18–078

Illustration 7. Were the divorce granted after March 1, 2001, it, being granted in another Member State of the European Union, would now be recognised in England on that basis: Council Regulation 1347/2000, Arts 13(1), 14(1).

18–084

A talak pronounced in Lebanon was recognised under section 46(1) of the Family Law Act 1986. The requirement to register the talak after the event in a Sharia court was held sufficient to constitute proceedings. The test was said to be "whether the divorce depends for its validity, at least in part, on what can properly be termed 'proceedings' " : the effect of the words "at least in part" is obscure: *El Fadl v. El Fadl* [2000] 1 F.L.R. 175.

18–094

Illustrations 1, 2 and 4. The decree, being granted in another Member State of the European Union, would now be recognised in England on that basis: Council Regulation 1347/2000, Arts 13(1), 14(1).

18–109

Rule 82 does not apply to divorces, annulments of marriage or judicial separations pronounced in other Member States of the European Union. See Rule 82A. Denmark is not a Member State for the purposes of the Regulation: Art. 1(3).

18R–111

NOTE 34. See *El Fadl v. El Fadl* [2000] 1 F.L.R. 175 (no need for advance notice in case of Lebanese talak).

18–118

The observation in the text, that it is unclear what policy is served by requiring an official document, was referred to with evident approval in *Wicken v. Wicken* [1999] Fam. 224, where a foreign divorce was recognised despite the absence of documentation.

18–119

A divorce granted by a court in Northern Cyprus (under the auspices of the "Turkish Republic of Northern Cyprus", an entity not recognised by the United Kingdom) was refused recognition on grounds of public policy: *B. v. B. (Divorce: Northern Cyprus)* [2000] 2 F.L.R. 707, distinguishing *Carl Zeiss Stiftung v. Rayner & Keeler Ltd. (No. 2)* [1967] 1 A.C. 853 as a case dealing solely with private rights. See also entry at para. 25–004, *post*.

18–120

NOTE 48. Add: *El Fadl v. El Fadl* [2000] 1 F.L.R. 175.

18–121

18–123   Illustrations 1, 2 and 4. Were similar facts to lead to the grant of a divorce after March 1, 2001, the court would now be obliged to refuse recognition: Council Regulation 1347/2000, Art. 15(1); see Rule 82A.

18R–125   Insert new material:

RULE 82A—A divorce, annulment or legal separation entitled to recognition under Rule 78A must be refused recognition in England

(a) **if such recognition is manifestly contrary to English public policy; or**

(b) **where it was given in default of appearance, if the respondent was not served with the document which instituted the proceedings or with an equivalent document in sufficient time and in such a way as to enable the respondent to arrange for his or her defence unless it is determined that the respondent has accepted the judgment unequivocally; or**

(c) **if it is irreconcilable with a judgment given in English proceedings between the same parties; or**

(d) **if it is irreconcilable with an earlier judgment given in another Member State or in a non-Member State between the same parties, provided that the earlier judgment fulfils the conditions necessary for its recognition in England** (Art. 15(1))

COMMENT

The Rule states the effect of Article 15(1) of Council Regulation 1347/2000, which sets out the grounds on which divorces, annulments of marriage or judicial separations pronounced in other Member States must be refused recognition. The provisions of the Regulation apply only to legal proceedings instituted, to documents formally drawn up or registered as authentic instruments and to settlements which have been approved by a court in the course of proceedings after March 1, 2001 (Art. 42(1)). In each case, refusal of recognition is mandatory and is not a matter on which the English court has a discretion. Subject to that, ground (a) corresponds to Family Law Act 1986, s. 51(3)(*c*), as to which see para. 18–120. However, the test of public policy may not be applied to the rules relating to jurisdiction (Art. 17). Ground (b) raises similar issues to those in Family Law Act 1986, s. 51(3)(*a*), as to which see para. 18–115. Grounds (c) and (d) raise similar issues to those addressed in Family Law Act 1986, s.51(1), as to which see para. 18–113.

Article 16 of the Regulation enables a Member State to enter into agreements with non-Member States under which the Member State will not recognise judgments pronounced elsewhere in the European Union where jurisdiction to give that judgment could only have been on grounds of jurisdiction other than those specified in Articles 2 to 7, in other words it was a case of "residual jurisdiction" under Article 8 applying national law. (*Cf.* para. 14–204 for the similar case under the Brussels or Lugano Conventions.)

The jurisdiction of the court of the Member State of origin may not be reviewed (Art. 17). The recognition of a judgment relating to a divorce, legal separation or an annulment of marriage may not be refused because English law would not allow divorce, judicial separation or annulment on the same facts (Art. 18). Under no circumstances may a judgment be reviewed as to its substance (Art. 19). If recognition is sought in England of a judgment given in another Member State the court may stay the proceedings if an ordinary appeal against the judgment has been lodged (Art. 20(1)). If the judgment was given in Ireland, the English court may stay the proceedings if enforcement is suspended in Ireland by reason of an appeal (Art. 20(2)).

4. FINANCIAL RELIEF

A. *Jurisdiction of the English courts*

The English court is unlikely to grant leave where the applicant is essentially seeking to enforce a foreign order for financial provision and has not exhausted other methods of enforcement: *Jordan v. Jordan* [1999] 2 F.L.R. 1069 (C.A.). The Court of Appeal in that case held that it was not essential that the applicant establish hardship, rejecting a suggestion to that effect in *N. v. N. (Foreign Divorce: Financial Relief)* [1997] 1 F.L.R. 900.

18–163

Maintenance Orders (Facilities for Enforcement) Act 1920, s. 4(5B)(6A) is amended by Access to Justice Act 1999, s. 90(1), Sched. 13, para 7(1), (2) (3)(a), Sched. 15, Pt V, Table (7) (not yet in force).

18–174

The clerk of the justices will become the justices' chief executive when amendments to Maintenance Orders (Reciprocal Enforcement) Act 1972, s. 26(6) made by Access to Justice Act 1999, s. 90(1), Sched. 13, paras 71, 76 are brought into force.

18–182

The clerk of the justices will become the justices' chief executive when amendments to Maintenance Orders (Reciprocal Enforcement) Act 1972, ss. 27 and 32 made by Access to Justice Act 1999, s 90(1), Sched. 13 are brought into force.

18–183

5. STAYING OF MATRIMONIAL PROCEEDINGS

With effect from March 1, 2001, when Council Regulation 1347/2000 (as to which see para. 18R–001) comes into force, Rule 89(2) will be subject to the following new sub-rule:

18R–227

(3) Where the jurisdiction of the English court is derived from Council Regulation 1347/2000 and
(i) proceedings involving the same cause of action and between the same parties have been brought in England and in another Member State, or
(ii) proceedings for divorce, legal separation or annulment of marriage not involving the same cause of action and between the same parties are brought in England and in another Member State,
and the courts of the other Member State were seised first, the court must of its own motion stay the English proceedings until such time as the jurisdiction of the court first seised is established; and where the jurisdiction of the court first seised is established, the court must decline jurisdiction (Regulation, Art. 11(1)(2)(3). Denmark is not a Member State for the purposes of the Regulation: Art. 1(3)).
For this purpose, a court is seised (a) at the time when the document instituting the proceedings or an equivalent document is lodged with the court, provided that the applicant has not subsequently failed to take the steps he was required to take to have service effected on the respondent; or (b) if the

document has to be served before being lodged with the court, at the time when it is received by the authority responsible for service, provided that the applicant has not subsequently failed to take the steps he was required to take to have the document lodged with the court (*ibid*. Art. 11(4)). The provisions of the Regulation apply only to legal proceedings instituted after March 1, 2001 (Art. 42(1)).

18–231   NOTE 50. Add: *Krenge v. Krenge* [1999] 1 F.L.R. 969 (German forum advantageous to one party, but stay on basis that it is the natural forum).

CHAPTER 19

CHILDREN

2. GUARDIANSHIP AND CUSTODY

A. *Jurisdiction of the English court*

The 1998 Convention (as to which see para. 19–034) never came into force, **19R–011**
and was overtaken by the extension of the competence of the European
institutions by the Treaty of Amsterdam's establishment of an "area of
freedom, security and justice". The draft Convention was converted, with
modifications, into a Regulation, Council Regulation 1347/2000 of 29 May
2000 on jurisdiction and the recognition and enforcement of judgments in
matrimonial matters and in matters of parental responsibility for children of
both spouses (for text see [2000] O.J. L160) binding on Member States and
coming into force on March 1, 2001. The provisions of the Regulation apply
only to legal proceedings instituted after March 1, 2001 (Art. 42(1)). Sub-rule
(3) is subject to an additional Proviso:

**And provided that where the English court is exercising jurisdiction on
an application for divorce, judicial separation or nullity of marriage
under Article 2 of Council Regulation 1347/2000, it has jurisdiction in a
matter relating to parental responsibility over a child of both spouses if,
and only if,**
    (i) the child is habitually resident in England; or
    **(ii) the child is not habitually resident in England, but is habitually
resident in one of the Member States and (a) at least one of the spouses
has parental responsibility in relation to the child; and (b) the jurisdiction
of the English courts has been accepted by the spouses and is in the best
interests of the child** (Regulation, Arts 3(1)(2), 7, 41; Denmark is not a
Member State for the purposes of the Regulation: Art. 1(3)).

The Regulation does not define the concept of "matters relating to parental
responsibility". This jurisdiction must be exercised in conformity with the
Hague Convention on the Civil Aspects of International Child Abduction, and
in particular Articles 3 and 16 thereof (Art. 4). This prevents decisions on the
merits of a custody application being taken where an application under the
Hague Convention is pending or imminent (see para. 19–100). Jurisdiction
under the Regulation ceases as soon as (a) the judgment allowing or refusing
the application for divorce, judicial separation or nullity of marriage has
become final; or (b) in those cases where proceedings in relation to parental
responsibility are still pending on that date, a judgment in these proceedings
has become final; or (c) the proceedings referred to in (a) and (b) have come
to an end for another reason (Art. 3(3)).

Insert a new sub-rule (7A):

**(7A) Where the jurisdiction of the English court is derived from Council
Regulation 1347/2000 and proceedings involving the same cause of action
and between the same parties have been brought in England and in**

another Member State, and the courts of the other Member State were seised first, the court must of its own motion stay the English proceedings until such time as the jurisdiction of the court first seised is established; and where the jurisdiction of the court first seised is established, the court must decline jurisdiction (Regulation, Art. 11(1)(2)(3). Denmark is not a Member State for the purposes of the Regulation: Art. 1(3)).

For this purpose, a court is seised (a) at the time when the document instituting the proceedings or an equivalent document is lodged with the court, provided that the applicant has not subsequently failed to take the steps he was required to take to have service effected on the respondent; or (b) if the document has to be served before being lodged with the court, at the time when it is received by the authority responsible for service, provided that the applicant has not subsequently failed to take the steps he was required to take to have the document lodged with the court (*ibid.* Art. 11(4)).

19–031   If courts in England and in another part of the United Kingdom are both seised of divorce proceedings and applications for orders relating to a child are made in both sets of proceedings, the English court will resolve the matter by reference to the rules as to staying matrimonial proceedings in Schedule 1 to the Domicile and Matrimonial Proceedings Act 1987, stated in Rule 89: *A. v. A. (Forum Conveniens)* [1999] 1 F.L.R. 1.

19–038   The jurisdictional rules were given an extended meaning by Singer J. in *Re P. (A Child: Mirror Orders)* [2000] 1 F.L.R. 435. A United States court was prepared to allow a child to travel to England on condition that a "mirror order" was made by the English court to ensure the child's return. The English courts have often adopted a similar practice. The child in the instant case was neither habitually resident nor present in England. Nonetheless an order was made on the basis of "common sense, comity and public policy"; it was expressly limited to the period during which the child was present in England. The convenience of the outcome is clear, but it is not in accordance with the jurisdictional rules in the Family Law Act 1986.

19–047   A court considering the possible removal of a child from the jurisdiction will not generally interfere with what it regards as a reasonable decision by the custodial parent: *Re H. (Application to Remove from Jurisdiction)* [1998] 1 F.L.R. 848 (C.A.); *Re K. (Application to remove Children from Jurisdiction)* [1998] 2 F.L.R. 1006: *Re C. (Leave to Remove from Jurisdiction)* [2000] 2 F.L.R. 457 (C.A.). This practice does not conflict with Article 8 of the European Convention on Human Rights: *Re A. (Permission to Remove Child from Jurisdiction)* [2000] 2 F.L.R. 225 (C.A.).

NOTE 47. The court may require steps to be taken to ensure the return of the child, *e.g.* the taking of oaths on the Koran before a Sharia judge in Saudi Arabia before the child was taken there for a holiday by its mother, who was separated from the father: *Re A. (Security for Return to Jurisdiction)* [1999] 2 F.L.R. 1; *Re T. (Staying Contact in Non-Convention Country)* [1999] 1 F.L.R. 262n. (notarised agreement and mirror order of Cairo court required before child could travel to Egypt); *Re S. (Removal from Jurisdiction)* [1999] 1 F.L.R. 850 (exequatur in foreign court of English order and bond of £135,000 pending such action before child could go to Chile). The principles applied are the same, whether the application is under Children Act 1989, s. 13(1) (where a residence order is in force, see para. 19–045) or under 1989 Act, s. 8: *Re M. (Leave to Remove Child from Jurisdiction)* [1999] 2 F.L.R. 334. Because cases of this type may involve a sensitive examination of practice in foreign legal systems, they should be heard by a Family Division judge: *Re K. (Removal from Jurisdiction)* [1999] 2 F.L.R. 1084 (C.A.).

B. *Effect of foreign guardianship and custody orders*

NOTE 56. Add: *Re AGN (Adoption: Foreign Adoption)* [2000] 2 F.L.R. 431.   **19–051**

From March 1, 2001, in Rule 94(1) after "1985" insert "and to Council   **19R–058** Regulation 1347/2000 of May 29, 2000 on jurisdiction and the recognition and enforcement of judgments in matrimonial matters and in matters of parental responsibility for children of both spouses". See para. 19–066.

Abduction is not always by one parent. See *Re KR (Abduction: Forcible*   **19–062** *Removal by Parents)* [1999] 4 All E.R. 954, where a girl, taken by her parents to India against her will with a view to an arranged marriage, was returned after having been made a ward of court in England by her sister.

NOTE 8. Add to first sentence: *Re Z. (A Minor) (Abduction: Non-Convention*   **19–064** *Country)* [1999] 1 F.L.R. 1270. In *Osman v. Elisha* [2000] Fam. 62 (C.A.), the return of children to Sudan was ordered: the court was satisfied that the courts there applied a welfare principle, although it would be applied in the context of cultural and religious norms which differed from those prevailing in England. The court rejected the suggestion that *Re M. (Abduction: Peremptory Return Order)* [1996] 1 F.L.R. 478 (C.A.) was decided *per incuriam*: that case had "a legitimate place in the stream of authority".

NOTE 10. The making of orders requiring solicitors to disclose the where-   **19–065** abouts of their client or the client's child creates conflicting duties and is a limitation on legal professional privilege. The power will be exercised with sensitivity to this fact: *Re B. (Abduction: Disclosure)* [1995] 2 F.C.R. 601 (C.A.); *Re H. (Whereabouts Order to Solicitors)* [2000] 1 F.L.R. 766.

Council Regulation 1347/2000. The 1998 Convention never came into force,   **19–066** and was overtaken by the extension of the competence of the European institutions by the Treaty of Amsterdam's establishment of an "area of freedom, security and justice". The draft Convention was converted, with modifications, into a Regulation, Council Regulation 1347/2000 of May 29, 2000 on jurisdiction and the recognition and enforcement of judgments in matrimonial matters and in matters of parental responsibility for children of both spouses (for text see [2000] O.J. L160) binding on Member States and coming into force on March 1, 2001. In relations between Member States, the Regulation takes precedence over a number of multilateral Conventions in so far as they concern matters governed by the Regulation (Art. 37). They include the European Convention of May 20, 1980 on Recognition and Enforcement of Decisions concerning Custody of Children and on Restoration of Custody of Children (as to which, see para. 19–067). The provisions of the Regulation apply only to legal proceedings instituted, to documents formally drawn up or registered as authentic instruments and to settlements which have been approved by a court in the course of proceedings after March 1, 2001 (Art. 42(1)).

Chapter III of Council Regulation 1347/2000 contains provisions for the recognition and enforcement of judgments pronounced in the courts of other Member States. Denmark is not a Member State for the purposes of the Regulation: Art. 1(3). "Judgment" is defined to include a judgment relating to the parental responsibility of the spouses given on the occasion of proceedings for divorce, legal separation or annulment of marriage, whatever the judgment may be called, including a decree, order or decision (Art. 13(1). For jurisdiction, see para. 19R–011). Documents which have been formally drawn up or registered as authentic instruments and which are enforceable in a Member State, and settlements which have been approved by a court in the course of proceedings and are enforceable in the Member State in which they were concluded, are subject to the same rules as to recognition and enforcement as judgments (Art. 13(3)).

A judgment relating to the parental responsibility of the spouses given on the occasion of proceedings for divorce, legal separation or annulment of marriage will be recognised in England without any special procedure (Arts. 13(2), 14(1)). Where the recognition of a judgment is raised as an incidental question in a court of a Member State, that court may determine that issue (Art. 14(4)). However, the issue of recognition or non-recognition may also be raised by "any interested party" using the procedures prescribed in the Regulation for the enforcement of judgments (Art. 14(3); see below).

With regard to a Member State in which two or more systems of law or sets of rules concerning matters governed by the Regulation apply in different territorial units, (a) any reference to habitual residence in that Member State refers to habitual residence in a territorial unit; (b) any reference to nationality, or in the case of the United Kingdom "domicile", refers to the territorial unit designated by the law of that State; (c) any reference to the authority of a Member State having received an application for divorce or legal separation or for marriage annulment refers to the authority of a territorial unit which has received such an application; and (d) any reference to the rules of the requested Member State refers to the rules of the territorial unit in which jurisdiction, recognition or enforcement is invoked (Art. 41).

Grounds for non-recognition. However, the English court must not recognise a judgment (a) if such recognition is manifestly contrary to English public policy; or (b) if it was given, except in case of urgency, without the child having been given an opportunity to be heard, in violation of fundamental principles of English procedure; or (c) where it was given in default of appearance if the person in default was not served with the document which instituted the proceedings or with an equivalent document in sufficient time and in such a way as to enable that person to arrange for his or her defence unless it is determined that such person has accepted the judgment unequivocally; or (d) on the request of any person claiming that the judgment infringes his or her parental responsibility, if it was given without such person having been given an opportunity to be heard; or (e) if it is irreconcilable with a later judgment relating to parental responsibility given in the Member State in which recognition is sought; or (f) if it is irreconcilable with a later judgment relating to parental responsibility given in another Member State or in the non-Member State of the habitual residence of the child provided that the later judgment fulfils the conditions necessary for its recognition in England (Art. 15(2). *Cf.* Rule 82A, setting out the rules for the non-recognition of divorces, legal separations and annulments.)

Article 16 of the Regulation enables a Member State to enter into agreements with non-Member States under which the Member State will not recognise judgments pronounced elsewhere in the European Union where jurisdiction to give that judgment could only have been on grounds of jurisdiction other than those specified in Articles 2 to 7, in other words it was a case of "residual jurisdiction" under Article 8 applying national law. (*Cf.* para. 14–204 for the similar case under the Brussels or Lugano Conventions.)

The jurisdiction of the court of the Member State of origin may not be reviewed (Art. 17). The recognition of a judgment relating to a divorce, legal separation or an annulment of marriage may not be refused because English law would not allow divorce, judicial separation or annulment on the same facts (Art. 18). Under no circumstances may a judgment be reviewed as to its substance (Art. 19). If recognition is sought in England of a judgment given in another Member State the court may stay the proceedings if an ordinary appeal against the judgment has been lodged (Art. 20(1)). If the judgment was given in Ireland, the English court may stay the proceedings if enforcement is suspended in Ireland by reason of an appeal (Art. 20(2)).

Enforcement. A judgment on the exercise of parental responsibility in respect of a child of both parties given in a Member State which is enforceable in that Member State and has been served must be enforced in England when, on the application of any interested party, it has been registered for enforcement in England (Art. 21(1)(2)). An application for a declaration of enforceability must be made to the High Court (Art. 22 and Annex I). The procedure is a matter for the *lex fori* (Art. 23(1); but see Arts. 23(2)(3), 32–35 as to representation and documents, Art. 25 as to notification of the decision, Art. 30 as to legal aid, and Art. 31 as to security for costs). The High Court is required to give its decision without delay. The person against whom enforcement is sought is not at this stage of the proceedings entitled to make any submissions on the application (Art. 24(1)). The application may be refused only for one of the reasons specified in Articles 15, 16 and 17 (Art. 24(2); for Arts 15, 16, and 17, see above: Art. 17 in fact contains no ground for refusal). Under no circumstances may a judgment be reviewed as to its substance (Art. 24(3)). An applicant may request partial enforcement of a judgment. Where a judgment has been given in respect of several matters and enforcement cannot be authorised for all of them, the court must authorise partial enforcement (Art. 29).

Either party may appeal against the decision to the High Court (see Art. 26 and Annex II; rules of court will determine how the appeal is to be heard). The judgment given on appeal may be contested only by a single further appeal on a point of law (Art. 27 and Annex III. See Art. 28 for suspension pending appeal in the Member State of origin).

Text to note 15. The inconvenience sometimes resulting from the need to deal **19–067** with an application under the Hague Convention before an accompanying application under the European Convention was the subject of comment in *Re D. (Abduction: Discretionary Return)* [2000] 1 F.L.R. 24.

NOTE 19. For parties, see now S.I. 2000 No. 1107. **19–068**

In exceptional circumstances, a child may be separately represented in pro- **19–069** ceedings under the European Convention: *Re T. (Abduction: Appointment of Guardian ad Litem)* [1999] 2 F.L.R. 796. *Cf.* the practice under the Hague Convention: below, para. 19–094.

19–072 NOTE 30. Add: *S.D. v. R.S. (Child Abduction)* [1996] 3 I.R. 524.

NOTE 31. Add: *Re T. (Abduction: Child's Objections to Return)* [2000] 2 F.L.R. 192.

NOTE 38. In *Re L. (Abduction: European Convention: Access)* [1999] 2 F.L.R. 1089, the fact that the foreign court proceeded under a misapprehension as to the country in which the child was then living was treated as a "change of circumstances"; *sed quaere.*

19–076 See Beaumont and McEleavy, *The Hague Convention on International Child Abduction* (1999).

NOTE 52. For parties, see now S.I. 2000 No. 1107.

NOTE 56. Add: *Re H. (Abduction: Child of 16)* [2000] 2 F.L.R. 51 (age at date of hearing decisive).

19–077 See Beaumont and McEleavy, *The Hague Convention on International Child Abduction* (1999), Chap. 7.

NOTE 59. Add: *Re H. (Abduction: Habitual Residence: Consent)* [2000] 2 F.L.R. 294 (where parents held to be habitually resident in different countries); *Re N. (Abduction: Habitual Residence)* [2000] 2 F.L.R. 899 (similar facts).

19–078 NOTE 63. Add: *Re V-B. (Abduction: Custody Rights)* [1999] 2 F.L.R. 192 (C.A.) (right under Dutch law to be informed of and consulted as to major decisions affecting child held not to amount to "rights of custody").

NOTE 64. The point discussed in the note was clarified by the House of Lords in *Re H. (Child Abduction: Rights of Custody)* [2000] 2 A.C. 291 (where the rights of custody were held to be vested in a foreign court). Although in one case (*Re S. (Abduction: Separate Representation of Children* [1997] 2 F.C.R. 342) a foreign court had been represented, it was proper, and generally more appropriate, for the application for the return of the child to be made by the parent whose application to the foreign court had given that court rights of custody. In *Re JS (Private International Adoption)* [2000] 2 F.L.R. 638, the rights were vested in an adoption agency in Texas which successfully applied for the return of the child by the prospective adopters in England.

Text to notes 65 to 67. That a court could be an "institution or body" possessing rights of custody for the purposes of the Convention was affirmed by the House of Lords in *Re H. (Child Abduction: Rights of Custody)* [2000] 2 W.L.R. 337, where the relevant cases are reviewed. In *Re C. (Abduction: Wrongful Removal)* [1999] 2 F.L.R. 859, Hale J. held that a court could have rights of custody for the purposes of the Convention when it was actively seised of an application for a parental responsibility order, and rejected the view of the Child Abduction Unit expressed in the *Practice Note* of 1998. She reached a similar conclusion in *Re J. (Abduction: Rights of Custody)* [1999] 2 F.L.R. 653 (affirmed on grounds unrelated to this point, [2000] 1 F.L.R. 78 (C.A.)), where applications had been made for both a parental responsibility order and a prohibited steps order. These developments were noted by the Court of Appeal in *Re H. (Child Abduction: Rights of Custody)* [2000] 1 F.L.R 201, where Thorpe L.J. offered some further guidance. An application for contact would not vest rights of custody in a court, but one dealing with the physical care of the child or with parental responsibility might do so. It was necessary to scrutinise the nature of the application, its merits, and the commitment of the applicant to its pursuit. The House of Lords, in dismissing a further appeal, merely observed that the application must raise matters of custody within the meaning of the Convention and that required in each case a consideration of the terms of the application. The House also held that the court would be vested with rights of custody in appropriate cases from the time the document initiating the proceedings is served until the proceedings were stayed or disposed of: [2000] 2 A.C. 291.

NOTE 74. The argument that under the law of Zimbabwe, the country of habitual residence, the separation of the parents gave all custody rights to the mother, so that her removal of the child could not be wrongful in terms of the Convention, was rejected in *Re D. (Abduction: Custody Rights)* [1999] 2 F.L.R. 626. Allowing the domestic law of the country of habitual residence to determine the issue in that way would effectively "negative" the Convention. For criticism of *Re F. (A Minor) (Abduction: Custody Rights Abroad)* [1995] Fam. 224 (C.A.), see Beaumont and McEleavy, *The Hague Convention on International Child Abduction* (1999), pp. 62–63.   **19–080**

NOTE 79. Add: Beaumont and McEleavy, *The Hague Convention on International Child Abduction* (1999), pp. 58–61. *Re B. (A Minor) (Abduction)* [1994] 2 F.L.R. 249 (C.A.) was not followed by the Irish Supreme Court in *HI. v. MG.* [1999] 2 I.L.R.M. 1: the admitted difficulties in dealing satisfactorily with the claims of unmarried fathers were best dealt with through the machinery of the Hague Conference and not by "innovative judicial responses", producing results which could not have been contemplated by the authors of the Convention.

NOTE 88. Add: Beaumont and McEleavy, *The Hague Convention on International Child Abduction* (1999), pp. 55–56.   **19–082**

Text to note 98. It was held in *Re L. (Abduction: Pending Criminal Proceedings)* [1999] 1 F.L.R. 433 that return does not have to be to the State from which the child was abducted (in that case, re-abducted).   **19–084**

In *Re P. (Abduction: Minor's Views)* [1998] 2 F.L.R. 825 (C.A.), Butler-Sloss L.J. said that the courts were "rightly sceptical of attempts by many abducting parents to invoke the provisions of Article 13 to try to stave off the almost inevitable requirement to return the child forthwith to the state of habitual residence. The welfare of the child who has been abducted is generally seen as best served by returning him to the jurisdiction of his habitual residence and leaving the decision of what should happen to him thereafter to the court best equipped to deal with the custodial problems of the family living within its jurisdiction before the child was abducted".   **19–087**

NOTE 8. Oral evidence was taken, but this was regarded as unusual, in *Re M. (Abduction: Leave to Appeal)* [1999] 2 F.L.R. 550 (C.A.). Orders should not be made that one issue be dealt with as a preliminary point of law, as this can lead to delay: the case should be dealt with on one occasion if at all possible: *HI. v. MG.* [1999] 2 I.L.R.M. 1 (Sup. Ct.).

NOTE 10. Add: *Re M. (Abduction) (Consent: Acquiescence)* [1999] 1 F.L.R. 171.   **19–089**

NOTE 12. In *Re M. (Abduction) (Consent: Acquiescence)* [1999] 1 F.L.R. 171, Wall J. retracted the view he had expressed in *Re W. (Abduction: Procedure)* [1995] 1 F.L.R. 878 that consent would normally be in writing.

19–090   Text to note 13. In *T. v. T. (Child Abduction: Consent)* [1999] 2 F.L.R. 912, Charles J. held that consent could be vitiated by misunderstanding or non-disclosure. In the instant case, the mother had obtained the apparent consent of the father to her bringing the child to England, but it was held that the consent was vitiated by her failure to disclose to the father her sexual relationship with another man in England. It is submitted that this decision goes considerably further than was required either by earlier authority or sound policy, as opening the door to allegations of incomplete disclosure of the full circumstances.

NOTE 15. Add at end: *Re I. (Abduction: Acquiescence)* [1999] 1 F.L.R. 778.

NOTE 18. Add at end: *Re B. (Abduction: Acquiescence)* [1999] 2 F.L.R. 818.

19–091   NOTE 26. *Re R. (Minors) (Abduction: Consent)* is now reported *sub nom. Re R. (Abduction: Consent)* [1999] 1 F.L.R. 828.

NOTE 28. Although the reference to a stringent test in *Re F. (A Minor) (Abduction: Custody Rights Abroad)* [1995] Fam. 224 (C.A.) was approved in *Re C. (Abduction: Grave Risk of Psychological Harm)* [1999] 1 F.L.R 1145 (C.A.), the decision in *Re F.* was there characterised as the high water mark of cases in which return was refused on this ground. Add: *Pollastro v. Pollastro* (1999) 171 D.L.R. (4th) 32 (Ont. C.A.); *Finizio v. Scoppio-Finizio* (2000) 179 D.L.R. (4th) 713 (Alta.).

Text to note 29. This principle was applied in cases involving alleged sexual abuse of the child by the mother's cohabitee: *Re S. (Abduction: Return into Care)* [1999] 1 F.L.R. 843; and the murder by the father (who was shortly to be released from prison) of a man he suspected of having had an affair with the abducting mother: *Re M. (Abduction: Intolerable Situation)* [2000] 1 F.L.R. 930.

NOTE 30. In *Re C. (Abduction: Grave Risk of Physical or Psychological Harm)* [1999] 2 F.L.R. 478 (C.A.), the Court of Appeal emphasised that little weight could be given to an abducting parent's self-induced dilemma.

19–092   It is not appropriate for an English court to consider allegations that a court in another Hague Convention country will not give the abducting parent a fair hearing: *Re S. (Abduction: Intolerable Situation: Beth Din)* [2000] 1 F.L.R. 454.

19–093   In some cases, direct communication between the English court and the judicial or other authorities of the relevant foreign country may be an alternative to, or complement, the taking of undertakings: *Re M. and J. (Abduction: International Judicial Collaboration)* [2000] 1 F.L.R. 803.

19–094   NOTE 44. Add: *Re T. (Abduction: Child's Objections to Return)* [2000] 2 F.L.R. 192 (child of 11 had cogent fears concerning his mother's drink problem).

NOTE 49. Add: *Re T. (Abduction: Child's Objections to Return)* [2000] 2 **19–095**
F.L.R. 192.

Text to note 51. The apparent assumption in *Re H. (Abduction: Child of 16)* **19–096**
[2000] 2 F.L.R. 51 that the 12 months could be taken to run from the date on
which the whereabouts of the abducting parent and child become known to the
other parent cannot be reconciled with the words of Article 12.

NOTE 54. Insofar as *In the Marriage of Graziano and Daniels* [1991] F.L.C.
92–212 adds an unnecessary gloss on the plain meaning of the term "settled",
it should not be followed: *Townsend v. Director-General, Department of
Families, Youth and Community Care* [1999] F.L.C. 92–842. For an illustration of the approach adopted in cases of claimed settlement, see *P. v. B.*
(unreported, Irish Supreme Court, February 26, 1999).

The European Court of Human Rights has held that the treatment of married **19–097**
and unmarried fathers under the Hague Convention has an objective and
reasonable justification and is not in conflict with Articles 8 and 14 of the
European Convention on Human Rights: *B. v. United Kingdom* [2000] 1
F.L.R. 1 (the case dealt with in the English courts as *Re B. (Abduction) (Rights
of Custody)* [1997] 2 F.L.R. 594 (C.A.)).

NOTE 57. For the similar practice in Scotland, see *Donofrio v. Burrell*, 2000 **19–098**
S.C.L.R. 465.

NOTE 67. See *Re M. (Abduction: Conflict of Jurisdiction)* [2000] 2 F.L.R. 372, **19–101**
illustrating in this context the interplay of the Hague and European
Conventions.

NOTE 68. In *Re L. (Abduction: Pending Criminal Proceedings)* [1999] 1
F.L.R. 433, a Danish court had ordered the return of a child to Florida under
the Hague Convention. The abducting parent removed the child to England.
The court held that the issue estoppel recognised in *Re O. (Child Abduction:
Re-Abduction)* [1997] 2 F.L.R. 712 was applicable, but on facts new issues
arose which required consideration.

CHAPTER 20

LEGITIMACY, LEGITIMATION AND ADOPTION

1. LEGITIMACY

A. *Jurisdiction of the English Court*

20R–001 With effect from the coming into force of section 83 of the Child Support, Pensions and Social Security Act 2000, delete "parentage or". See para. 20–004, below.

NOTE 2. Family Law Act 1986 is repealed by Child Support, Pensions and Social Security Act 2000, Sched. 9, Pt. X, but provision to the same effect is made by Family Law Act 1986, ss. 55, 56 both as amended by Child Support, Pensions and Social Security Act 2000, Sched. 8, paras. 4 and 5. These provisions are not yet in force.

20–004 Sections 56(1)(*a*) and 58(5)(*b*) of the Family Law Act 1986 are repealed by Child Support, Pensions and Social Security Act 2000, Sched. 9, Pt. X (not yet in force). Fresh provision is made for declarations of parentage by a new section 55A of the 1986 Act, inserted by 2000 Act, section 83 (not yet in force). This provides that the High Court, a county court or a magistrates' court has jurisdiction to make a declaration as to whether or not a person named in the application is or was the parent of another person so named if, and only if, either of the persons named in it (a) is domiciled in England and Wales on the date of the application; or (b) has been habitually resident in England and Wales throughout the period of one year ending with that date; or (c) died before that date and (i) was at death domiciled in England and Wales, or (ii) had been habitually resident in England and Wales throughout the period of one year ending with the date of death. The effect of the new provisions is to widen, with certain safeguards (see s. 55A(3)(5)), the range of persons who may seek declarations of parentage and to remove the earlier requirement that both parents had to be respondents. The changes will be of particular use in immigration contexts.

C. *Succession by and to Legitimate Persons*

20–036 Text to note 38. The House of Lords' Committee for Privileges has held that the limitation of succession to a peerage to legitimate persons does not offend Article 14 of the European Convention on Human Rights read with Article 1 of the First Protocol: *Re Moynihan* [2000] 1 F.L.R. 113, distinguishing *Inze v. Austria* (1987) 10 E.H.R.R. 394.

3. ADOPTION

A. *Jurisdiction of the English Courts*

20–100 In a number of cases involving inter-country adoptions the issue has arisen as to whether a foreign institution in which parental rights have been vested under the relevant foreign law can be recognised as a guardian for the purposes of consent under Adoption Act 1976, s. 16. Although it was held in *Re D. (Adoption: Foreign Guardianship)* [1999] 2 F.L.R. 865 that only an English institution qualified, the better view is that the foreign institution should be recognised, applying the principle stated in Rule 93: *Re AMR (Adoption: Procedure)* [1999] 2 F.L.R. 807; *Re AGN (Adoption: Foreign Adoption)* [2000] 2 F.L.R. 431.

Consent by a natural parent to adoption in the foreign country will not be treated as equivalent to consent to an adoption in England: *Re A. (Adoption of a Russian Child)* [2000] 1 F.L.R. 539 (on this point following, reluctantly, *Re G. (Foreign Adoption: Consent)* [1995] 2 F.L.R. 534, but dispensing with consent).

NOTE 28. *Re C. (Adoption: Legality)* is now reported *sub nom. Re C. (A Minor) (Adoption: Illegality)* [1999] Fam. 128.   **20–105**

Text to note 29. The English courts cannot ignore the benefit to the child of acquiring a right of abode in the United Kingdom: it is an aspect of the welfare of the child to which first consideration must be given under Adoption Act 1976, s. 6. The same principle does not apply if it is a benefit which will be enjoyed when the child is an adult rather than during childhood, and the public policy issues surrounding immigration control may have then have to be given precedence: *Re B. (Adoption Order: Nationality)* [1999] 2 A.C. 136 (where adoption order upheld on facts).

NOTE 30. *Re R. (A Minor) (Inter-Country Adoptions: Practice)* is now reported *sub nom. Practice Note (Inter-Country Adoptions)* [1999] 1 W.L.R. 1324.   **20–106**

NOTE 34. British Nationality Act 1981, s. 1(5)(6) is amended by Adoption (Intercountry Aspects) Act 1999, s. 7.   **20–107**

After Illustration 3, insert as a new Illustration: **20–110**
3A. H and W are domiciled in the Isle of Man and wish to adopt C, who is in the Isle of Man. The High Court, but no other English court, has jurisdiction (Adoption Act 1976, ss. 14(2), 62(3); *Re J. (Adoption Procedure: Isle of Man)* [2000] 2 F.L.R. 633).

B. *Recognition of Foreign Adoptions*

Adoption Act 1976, s. 72(2) is amended, to substitute "the British Islands" for "Great Britain," by Adoption (Intercountry Aspects) Act 1999, Sched. 2, para. 3(8) (not yet in force).   **20R–111**

NOTE 47. A new s. 38(1)(*cc*) is inserted in the Adoption Act 1976 by Adoption (Intercountry Aspects) Act 1999, s. 4(1) (not yet in force). The effect will be to enable adoptions under the Hague Convention of 1993 (see para. 20–154) to be recognised. However by a new s. 39(3A) (inserted by the 2000 Act, s. 4(3) (not yet in force)), a Convention adoption may be refused recognition, or given limited recognition, if it is not a "full" adoption (one in which the child ceases to be treated in law as the child of any person other than the adopters) and certain other conditions are met.

20–112 NOTE 52. Adoption Act 1976, s. 38 is amended by Adoption (Intercountry Aspects) Act 1999, s. 4(1) (not yet in force).

20–115 For the annulment of adoptions made under the Hague Convention of 1993, see para. 20–149, below.

20–127 Family Law Act 1986, s. 57(1) is amended by Adoption (Intercountry Aspects) Act 1999, Sched. 2, para. 5 (not yet in force) to enable declarations to be made in respect of the validity of Convention adoption orders made under the Hague Convention of 1993.

D. *Adoptions under the Hague Convention of 1965*

20–138 The Adoption (Intercountry Aspects) Act 1999 (the relevant provisions of which are not yet in force) will lead to the denunciation by the United Kingdom of the 1965 Convention and its effective replacement by the Hague Convention on Protection of Children and Co-operation in respect of Intercountry Adoption of 1993. Many of the provisions as to Convention adoptions in the Adoption Act 1976 (where, as originally enacted, the term referred to adoptions under the 1965 Convention) are adapted to apply to adoptions under the 1993 Convention.

20–140– A new text of section 17 of the Adoption Act 1976 is substituted by Adoption
147 (Intercountry Aspects) Act 1999, s. 3 (not yet in force). It enables an adoption order to be made in England as a Convention adoption order in circumstances to be prescribed by regulations.

20–148 Section 70 of the Adoption Act 1976 is repealed by Adoption (Intercountry Aspects) Act 1999, Sched. 3 (not yet in force).

20–149 A new text of section 53(1) of the Adoption Act 1976 is substituted by Adoption (Intercountry Aspects) Act 1999, s. 6(1) (not yet in force). It enables a Convention adoption order in the new sense of one made under the Hague Convention of 1993 to be annulled.

20–150 Fresh provision is made by Adoption (Intercountry Aspects) Act 1999, s. 6(4) (not yet in force) as to the effect of determinations and orders made in courts outside England in respect of Convention adoption orders in the new sense of one made under the Hague Convention of 1993. The terms "regulated adoption" and "specified order" cease to be used.

20–152 For the annulment of Convention adoption orders in the new sense of one made under the Hague Convention of 1993, see para. 20–149, above.

20–154 Section 1 of the Adoption (Intercountry Aspects) Act 1999 (not yet in force) enables regulations to be made to give effect to the 1993 Convention.

CHAPTER 21

MENTAL DISORDER

A Convention on the International Protection of Adults was agreed under the **21–002**
auspices of the Hague Conference on Private International Law in October
1999. It applies to the protection in international situations of adults who, by
reason of an impairment or insufficiency of their personal faculties, are not in
a position to protect their interests (Art. 1(1)). It deals with the questions
which State has jurisdiction to take measures directed to the protection of the
person or property of the adult; which law is to be applied in the exercise of
this jurisdiction; which law applies to the representation of the adult; and it
provides for the recognition and enforcement of such measures of protection
in other Contracting States (Art. 1(2)). The measures covered include "in
particular" (a) the determination of incapacity and the institution of a protective regime; (b) the placing of the adult under the protection of a judicial
or administrative authority; (c) guardianship, curatorship and analogous institutions; (d) the designation and functions of any person or body having charge
of the adult's person or property, representing or assisting the adult; (e) the
placement of the adult in an establishment or other place where protection can
be provided; (f) the administration, conservation or disposal of the adult's
property; and (g) the authorisation of a specific intervention for the protection
of the person or property of the adult (Art. 3).

The principal rule as to jurisdiction is that it lies with the judicial or
administrative authorities of the Contracting State of the habitual residence of
the adult (Art. 5(1)). The authorities of a Contracting State of which the adult
is a national have jurisdiction if they consider that they are in a better position
to assess the interests of the adult (Art. 7(1)). Other States may be requested
by the authorities of the State seised of the case to deal with aspects of the
adult's protection (Art. 8). The authorities of a Contracting State where
property of the adult is situated have jurisdiction to take measures of protection concerning that property, to the extent that such measures are compatible
with those taken by the authorities having jurisdiction under the main provisions of the Convention (Art. 9).

In exercising their jurisdiction under the Convention, the authorities of the
Contracting States are to apply their own law. However, in so far as the
protection of the person or the property of the adult requires, they may
exceptionally apply or take into consideration the law of another State with
which the situation has a substantial connection (Art. 13).

The measures taken by the authorities of a Contracting State are to be
recognised by operation of law in all other Contracting States (Art. 22(1)), but
the Convention sets out a number of grounds on which recognition may be
refused (Art. 22(2)). The Convention also contains detailed provisions as to
practical co-operation between the authorities of the different Contracting
States.

The Convention is not yet in force and has not been signed by the United
Kingdom.

CHAPTER 22

NATURE AND SITUS OF PROPERTY

22–026 Text at note 59. Order 11, r. 1 is replaced by CPR, rr. 6.19 and 6.20.

22–046 See entry at para. 22–026, *supra*.

22–061 NOTE 63. Air Navigation (No. 2) Order 1995 (S.I. 1995 No. 1970) was revoked and replaced by provisions of Air Navigation Order 2000 (S.I. 2000 No. 1562).

CHAPTER 23

IMMOVABLES

NOTE 6. Order 11, r. 1(1)(*g*) is replaced by CPR, r. 6.20(10).   **23R–001**

NOTE 7. To the extent that claims which fell within Order 11, r. 1(1)(*h*) are covered by CPR, r. 6.20, they are within paragraph 10 which permits service out if "the whole subject matter of a claim relates to property located within the jurisdiction."

Final sentence. The relevant part of Order 11 is replaced by CPR, r. 6.20.   **23–008**

Text at note 17. See entry at para. 23–008, *supra*.   **23–009**

NOTE 14. Order 11, r. 1(2) is replaced by CPR, r. 6.19.

NOTE 15. Order 11, r. 1(1) is replaced by CPR, r. 6.20.

In *Ashurst v. Pollard* [2001] 2 W.L.R. 722 (C.A.) it was held, on the basis of   **23–012**
Case C–294/92 *Webb* v. *Webb* [1994] E.C.R. I–1717, that the effect of Article 16(1) is not to deprive the English court of jurisdiction to make, on the application of the trustee in bankruptcy, an order requiring a bankrupt to sell land situated in Portugal.

In Case C–8/98 *Dansommer A/S* v. *Götz* [2000] E.C.R. I–393 a German   **23–013**
defendant took a holiday let of a house in Denmark from the plaintiff, a Danish company which acted as agent for the owner. The plaintiff alleged that the defendant had failed to clean the house properly before departure and had caused damage to the property. When the plaintiff started proceedings for damages against the defendant in Germany, a question arose as to whether the court had jurisdiction. In reply to the reference from the German court, the European Court ruled that Article 16(1)(a) is applicable to an action for damages for taking poor care of premises and causing damage to rented accommodation; Article 16(1)(a) applies to any proceedings concerning rights and obligations arising under an agreement for the letting of immovable property, irrespective of whether the action is based on a right *in rem* or a right *in personam*.

NOTE 73. Add: Briggs (1998) 69 B.Y.I.L. 356.   **23–027**

If a testator makes a will, leaving his house in Italy to his son, and then, prior   **23–045**
to his death, executes (in Ontario) a deed of gift of the same property to his daughters, the Ontario court does not have jurisdiction over the son's application have the deed of gift set aside. The deed (between the testator and his daughters) does not create any contractual or other legal obligation between the daughters and the son. See *Catania* v. *Giannattasio* (1999) 174 D.L.R. (4th) 170 (Ont. C.A.).

In *Hlynski* v. *Hlynski* (1999) 176 D.L.R. (4th) 132 (Sask. C.A.) the question arose as to whether, in the context of an application for a division of assets under the Matrimonial Property Act 1997 (Sask.), the courts of Saskatchewan were entitled to take into account the value of land in Manitoba (owned by the husband). The Saskatchewan Court of Appeal held that it did; either this aspect of the application fell outside the scope of the *Moçambique* rule (because the wife's claim to a share of the value of the land in Manitoba was not a claim to any title, right or interest in the Manitoba land itself) or it fell within one of the exceptions to the *Moçambique* rule (because it involved an equity running between the parties which indirectly affected land situated in Manitoba).

Chapter 24

PARTICULAR TRANSFERS OF MOVABLES

1. TRANSFER OF TANGIBLE THINGS

NOTE 3. Add: *Glencore International A.G. v. Metro Trading International Inc.* **24R–001**
[2001] 1 Lloyd's Rep. 284.

In *Glencore International A.G. v. Metro Trading International Inc., supra.* it **24–004**
was held that the *lex situs* applied generally to determine whether, and when,
property had passed, and was not displaced by the applicable law of the
transfer even as regards a dispute as to proprietary rights as between the
parties to the transfer.

NOTE 19. Add: *Glencore International A.G. v. Metro Trading International* **24–005**
Inc., supra.

In *Glencore International A.G. v. Metro Trading International Inc., supra*, the **24–007**
court examined, but found that it did not need to decide, the question whether
the *lex situs* was to be understood as a reference to the domestic law, or as
including the possibility of *renvoi* to another law.

Final sentence. This sentence was quoted with approval in *Glencore Inter-* **24–010**
national A.G. v. Metro Trading International Inc., supra, at p. 296

2. ASSIGNMENT OF INTANGIBLE THINGS

In *Raiffeisen Zentralbank Oesterreich A.G. v. Five Star General Trading* **24–048**
L.L.C. [2000] 1 All E.R. (Comm.) 897, the passage from "In relation . . . " to
the end of the page, and the passage in para. 24–049 from "The argument . . ."
to " . . . endowed by that law" were referred to with approval by Longmore
J. In that case, a claim was made by a mortgagee of a vessel, to whom all
insurance on the vessel had been assigned, seeking as against the owners of
the vessel, the insurers, and the owners of cargo aboard the vessel (who had
obtained attachment of the insurance and its proceeds in France), a declaration
that it was absolutely entitled to the proceeds of the insurance. Rejecting a
submission that these facts raised a proprietary question to which Article 12
of the Rome Convention was inapplicable, Longmore J. held that the true
issue was who, as against the insurer, was entitled to the insurance; and that
Article 12(2) of the Rome Convention referred this to English law as the law
governing the policy of insurance.

See also *Raiffeisen Zentralbank Oesterreich A.G. v. Five Star General Trading* **24–056**
L.L.C. [2000] 1 All E.R. (Comm.) 897.

CHAPTER 25

GOVERNMENTAL ACTS AFFECTING PROPERTY

25–004 See also *Kuwait Airways Corp. v. Iraqi Airways Co.* [2001] 1 Lloyd's Rep. 161 (C.A.) on the distinction between recognition of states and recognition of governments.

Text at note 21. In *Chen Li Hung v. Ting Lei Miao* [2000] H.K.L.R.D. 252, (2000) 3 H.K.C.F.A.R. 9 the Court of Final Appeal of Hong Kong accepted that where private rights, or acts of everyday occurrence, or perfunctory acts of administration were concerned, the courts might, in the interests of justice and common sense, where no consideration of public policy to the contrary prevailed, give recognition to the acts of an unrecognised government which was in *de facto* control. It was held that the Hong Kong courts will give effect to the orders of courts sitting in countries under the *de jure* sovereignty of the People's Republic of China but presently under the *de facto* (but unlawful) control of a usurper government, where: (i) the rights covered by those orders are private rights; (ii) giving effect to such orders accords with the interests of justice, the dictates of common sense and the needs of law and order; (iii) giving them effect would not be inimical to the interests of the People's Republic of China or otherwise contrary to public policy. Consequently the right of trustees in bankruptcy appointed by order of a Taiwanese court to recover the assets of the bankrupt in Hong Kong would be recognised, notwithstanding that the People's Republic of China regards Taiwan as part of, and under the *de jure* sovereignty of, the People's Republic of China, but as under the *de facto* and unlawful control of a usurper government. The rights were private. The action was not for the benefit of the government in Taiwan, but for the benefit of 100,000 Taiwanese private investors; and to give effect to the order would not involve recognition of the Taiwan regime or its courts.

In *B v. B (Divorce: Northern Cyprus)* [2000] 2 F.L.R. 707 a divorce granted by a court in the Turkish Republic of Northern Cyprus was not recognised, but the decision is not fully reasoned.

25–006 In *Kuwait Airways Corp. v. Iraqi Airways Co. (Nos. 4 and 5), supra*, the Court of Appeal expressed some sympathy with the view (but without actually deciding) that the *lex situs* rule might have no application where the property has been brought unlawfully into the territory of the confiscating state.

25–010 The decision in *Kuwait Airways Corp. v. Iraqi Airways Co. (No. 2)* [1999] C.L.C. 31 has been affirmed: *Kuwait Airways Corp. v. Iraqi Airways Co.* [2001] 1 Lloyd's Rep. 161 (C.A.), *ante*, paras. 5–038—5–041.

CHAPTER 27

SUCCESSION

The rule that the law of testator's domicile at the date of marriage determines **27–086**
whether that marriage operates to revoke the will was applied in *Allison v.*
Allison [1999] 3 W.W.R. 438 (B.C.), with the result that the law of British
Columbia (in which province the testator died domiciled) on the essential
validity of wills was inapplicable.

CHAPTER 29

TRUSTS

29–008 NOTE 26. Add: *Saliba v. Falzon* (N.S.W. Sup. Ct., 1998, unreported).

CHAPTER 30

CORPORATIONS AND CORPORATE INSOLVENCY

1. DOMICILE AND RESIDENCE

NOTE 8. In Case C–212/97 *Centros Ltd. v. Erhvervs-og Selskabsstyrelsen* **30–002**
[1999] E.C.R. I–1459, [2000] Ch. 446 the European Court held that it is
contrary to Articles 52 and 58 of the EC Treaty for a Member State to refuse
to register a branch of a company formed in accordance with the law of
another Member State in which it has its registered office but in which it
conducts no business, even where the branch is intended to enable the
company in question to carry on its entire business in the State in which the
branch is to be created, while avoiding the need to form a company there, thus
evading the application of the rules governing the formation of companies
which, in that State, are more restrictive as regards the paying up of a
minimum share capital. The European Court emphasized, however, that this
view did not prevent the authorities of the Member State concerned from
adopting any appropriate measure for preventing or penalising fraud either in
relation to the company itself (if necessary in co-operation with the Member
State in which the company was formed) or in relation to its members, where
it has been established that they are attempting, by means of the formation of
a company, to evade their obligations towards private or public creditors
established in the territory of the Member State concerned.

2. STATUS

NOTE 35. Add in line 12: *The Rio Assu* [1999] 1 Lloyd's Rep. 201; *J.H.* **30R–009**
Rayner (Mincing Lane) Ltd. v. Cafenorte S.A. Importadora [1999] 2 All E.R.
(Comm.) 577 (C.A.); *Eurosteel Ltd. v. Stinnes A.G.* [2000] 1 All E.R.
(Comm.) 964; *Astra S.A. Insurance and Reinsurance Co. v. Sphere Drake
Insurance Ltd.* [2000] 2 Lloyd's Rep. 550.

NOTE 44. Add in line 3: *The Rio Assu, supra*; *Astra S.A. Insurance and* **30–011**
Reinsurance Co. v. Sphere Drake Insurance Ltd., supra. See *Kuwait Airways
Corporation v. Iraqi Airways Co.* [2001] 1 Lloyd's Rep. 161 (C.A.), *ante*,
entry at paras. 5–038—5–041.

NOTE 46. See also *The Rio Assu, supra*; *Astra S.A. Insurance and Reinsurance
Co. v. Sphere Drake Insurance Ltd., supra*.

NOTE 51. Add in line 4: *The Rio Assu, supra*; *J.H. Rayner (Mincing Lane) Ltd.
v. Cafenorte S.A. Importadora, supra*; *Eurosteel Ltd. v. Stinnes A.G., supra*;
*Astra S.A. Insurance and Reinsurance Co. v. Sphere Drake Insurance Ltd.,
supra*.

NOTE 55. See also *Eurosteel Ltd. v. Stinnes A.G., supra*.

NOTE 74. Add: *Chen Li Hung v. Ting Lei Miao* [2000] 1 H.K.L.R.D. 252, **30–017**
(2000) 3 H.K.C.F.A.R. 9.

3. CAPACITY AND INTERNAL MANAGEMENT

30R–020 NOTE 76. In line 7 add: *Azov Shipping Co. v. Baltic Shipping Co.* [1999] 2 Lloyd's Rep. 159; *Grupo Torras S.A. v. Al-Sabah* [1999] C.L.C. 1469, revd. in part on other grounds [2001] C.L.C. 221 (C.A.).

NOTE 77. In line 10 add: *Azov Shipping Co. v. Baltic Shipping Co., supra*; *Grupo Torras S.A. v. Al-Sabah, supra.*

30–023 NOTE 85. Some discussion of these provisions can be found in *Azov Shipping Co. v. Baltic Shipping Co.* [1999] 2 Lloyd's Rep. 159, 170–173.

NOTE 87. It has been said that the expression "authority" in these provisions includes the doctrine of ostensible authority in a situation where the putative contract is governed by English law: see *Azov Shipping Co. v. Baltic Shipping Co., supra*, at p. 172.

30–024 NOTE 94. Add: *Azov Shipping Co. v. Baltic Shipping Co., supra.*

NOTE 96. Add: *Eurosteel Ltd. v. Stinnes A.G., supra.*

NOTE 97. Add: See also *Society of Lloyd's v. Fraser* [1998] C.L.C. 1630 (C.A.).

30–030 NOTE 24. Add: See also *Re Joseph Holt plc, The Times*, November 14, 2000.

4. WINDING UP

A. *Jurisdiction of English Courts*

30R–033 NOTE 33. The European Union Convention on Insolvency Proceedings has been replaced by Council Regulation (EC) 1346/2000 of May 29, 2000 on Insolvency Proceedings: See [2000] O.J. L160/1. See *post*, entry at paras. 30–132—139. Insolvency Act 2000, s. 14, in force from November 30, 2000, authorises the Secretary of State to make, by regulations, any provision which he considers necessary or expedient for the purpose of giving effect, with or without modifications, to the model law on cross-border insolvency, *i.e.* the model law contained in Annex I of the report of the 30th session of UNCITRAL: see *post*, entry at paras. 30–140—144.

NOTE 39. *Re Richbell Information Services Inc.* is now reported, *sub nom. Atlantic & General Investment Trust Ltd. v. Richbell Information Services Inc.* at [2000] B.C.C. 111. *Re Latreefers Inc.* [1999] 1 B.C.L.C. 271 has been affirmed *sub nom. Stocznia Gdanska S.A. v. Latreefers Inc., The Times*, March 15, 2000 (C.A.).

Add, in line 13: *Banco Nacional de Cuba v. Cosmos Trading Corp.* [2000] 1 B.C.L.C. 813 (C.A.).

30–036 NOTE 46. Order 11, r. 1(1) is replaced by CPR, r. 6.20.

30–041 NOTE 63. In line 2 add: *Banco Nacional de Cuba v. Cosmos Trading Corp.* [2000] 1 B.C.L.C. 813 (C.A.); *Stocznia Gdanska S.A. v. Latreefers Inc., The Times*, March 15, 2000 (C.A.).

30–044 NOTE 71. Re *Latreefers Inc.* [1999] 1 B.C.L.C. 271 has been affirmed *sub nom. Stocznia Gdanska S.A. v. Latreefers Inc., The Times*, March 15, 2000

(C.A.). *Re Richbell Information Services Inc.* is now reported, *sub nom. Atlantic & General Investment Trust Ltd. v. Richbell Information Services Inc.* at [2000] B.C.C. 111. Add: *Banco National de Cuba v. Cosmos Trading Corp.* [2000] 1 B.C.L.C. 813 C.A.) (although a winding-up order, if made, would enable liquidator to prosecute claims under Insolvency Act 1986, ss. 238 and 423, such claims would be against the Central Bank of Cuba which would be protected from them by State Immunity Act 1978, ss. 13 (2) and 14 (4): see main work, Chap. 10, para. 10–013: the mere "public relations benefit" of obtaining a winding-up order is not a benefit for these purposes).

The approach in *Re Real Estate Development Co.* [1991] B.C.L.C. 210 was   **30–046**
approved by the Court of Appeal in *Stocznia Gdanska S.A. v. Latreefers Inc., The Times*, March 15, 2000. The relevant principles consisted of three core requirements, namely (1) there must be a sufficient connection with England which may, but does not necessarily have to, consist of assets within the jurisdiction; (2) there must be a reasonable possibility, if a winding-up order is made, of benefit to those applying for the winding-up order; (3) one or more persons interested in the distribution of assets of the company must be persons over whom the court can exercise jurisdiction. In relation to the first requirement, it was stated in *Banco Nacional de Cuba v. Cosmos Trading Corp.* [2000] 1 B.C.L.C. 813, 819 (C.A.), that "the courts of this country should hesitate very long before subjecting foreign companies with no assets here to the winding-up procedures of this country". It was also stated (*ibid.*) that the making of an English winding-up order was generally undesirable where the foreign company continued to trade in its country of incorporation and elsewhere in the world and that the making of such an order in such a situation required exceptional circumstances and exceptional justification.

NOTE 81. *Re Latreefers Inc.* [1999] 1 B.C.L.C. 271 has been affirmed *sub*   **30–048**
nom. Stocznia Gdanska S.A. v. Latreefers Inc., The Times, March 15, 2000 (C.A.). *Re Richbell Information Services Inc.* is now reported, *sub nom. Atlantic & General Investment Trust Ltd. v. Richbell Information Services Inc.* at [2000] B.C.C. 111.

NOTE 74. Insolvency Act 1986, s. 426(10) (*a*), and (*b*) is amended by   **30–069**
Insolvency Act 2000, Sched. 4, Pt. II, para. 3. The amendments (which are not yet in force) do not affect the point made in the text to note 74.

B. *Effect of an English Winding-up Order*

NOTE 86. In *Banco Nacional de Cuba v. Cosmos Trading Corp.* [2000] 1   **30–072**
B.C.L.C. 813, 820 (C.A.) it was stated that it is something of a weakness in English winding-up law that it is not possible to have a winding-up of a foreign company limited to its activities and assets in England.

NOTE 13. See also *Banco Nacional de Cuba v. Cosmos Trading Corp., supra,*   **30–077**
at p. 819.

NOTE 38. See also *Banco Nacional de Cuba v. Cosmos Trading Corp., supra,*   **30–081**
at pp. 819–820.

NOTE 39. See previous entry.

30–084 NOTE 46. See also *Banco Nacional de Cuba v. Cosmos Trading Corp., supra*, at pp. 819–820.

30–086 NOTE 51 and text thereto. Company Directors' Disqualification Act 1986 is amended by Insolvency Act 2000, ss. 5–8 and Sched. 4, Pt. I. These amendments have not entered into force (*ibid.*, s. 16(1)) and do not affect the points made in the text.

C. *Effect of a Foreign Winding-up Order*

30–098 NOTE 6. Regulations made under the Insolvency Act 2000, s. 14, so as to implement the model law on cross-border insolvency (*ante*, entry at para. 30R–033, n. 33 and *post*, entry at paras. 30–140—144) may amend any provision of s. 426: Insolvency Act 2000, s. 14 (2)(*c*), in force from November 30, 2000. No such regulations have, as yet, been made.

30–100 NOTE 11. *England v. Purves* is now reported, *sub nom. Re J.N. Taylor Finance Pty. Ltd.* at [1999] 2 B.C.L.C. 256. Add: *Re Southern Equities Corp. Ltd., England v. Smith* [2000] 2 B.C.L.C. 21 (C.A.).

NOTES 12, 13. Insolvency Act 1982 s. 426 (10)(*a*) is amended by Insolvency Act 2000, Sched. 4, Pt. II (not yet in force). The amendments do not affect the point made in the text. The provisions of the Company Directors' Disqualification Act 1986 are amended by Insolvency Act 2000, ss. 5, 8 and Sched. 4, Pt. I (not yet in force).

NOTE 13 and text thereto. When applying the insolvency law of a relevant country or territory that corresponds to the insolvency law of England, the court should apply any principles, practices or discretions that the court requesting the assistance would apply in exercising its powers under the foreign law: *Re Southern Equities Corp. Ltd., England v. Smith* [2000] 2 B.C.L.C. 21 (C.A.), disapproving *Re J.N. Taylor Finance Pty. Ltd.* [1999] 2 B.C.L.C. 256. In *Re Southern Equities Corp. Ltd., England v. Smith, supra*, it was also held that application of the law of the requesting court should not be circumscribed by limitations to be found in the corresponding provisions of the insolvency law of England unless some principle of English public policy would be infringed were the foreign law to be applied according to its terms. Accordingly, the English court was prepared to accede to a request from the Supreme Court of South Australia seeking examination of a person allegedly concerned with the affairs of a company under section 596B of the Australian Corporations Law even though such an order would not have been made under the corresponding (but different) provisions of section 236 of the Insolvency Act 1986 because the order would be regarded as oppressive. Contrast *Re J.N. Taylor Finance Pty. Ltd., supra*, where such an order under the same section of the Australian law was denied because it would not have been granted under section 236 of the 1986 Act.

30–101 NOTE 27. *England v. Purves* is now reported, *sub nom. Re J.N. Taylor Finance Pty. Ltd.* at [1999] 2 B.C.L.C. 256. It was not followed in *Re Southern Equities Corp. Ltd., England v. Smith, supra*. See previous entry.

30–104 NOTE 31. As to *England v. Purves, The Times*, January 29, 1998, see previous entry. Add: *Re Southern Equities Corp. Ltd., England v. Smith, supra*.

NOTE 32. Add: *Re Southern Equities Corp. Ltd., England v. Smith, supra.*

NOTE 33. As to *England v. Purves, The Times,* January 29, 1998, see entry at para. 30–101, n. 27. Add: *Re Southern Equities Corp. Ltd., England v. Smith, supra.*

NOTE 34. Add: *Re Southern Equities Corp. Ltd., England v. Smith, supra.*

NOTE 35. As to *England v. Purves, The Times,* January 29, 1998, see entry at para. 30–101, n. 27. A request was granted in *Re Southern Equities Corp. Ltd., England v. Smith, supra.* See entry at para. 30–100, n. 3 and text thereto.

NOTES 38, 39. See also *Re Southern Equities Corp. Ltd., England v. Smith, supra.* **30–105**

NOTE 41. As to *England v. Purves, The Times,* January 29, 1998, see entry at para. 30–101, n. 27. Add: *Re Southern Equities Corp. Ltd., England v. Smith, supra.*

NOTE 49. As to *England v. Purves, The Times,* January 29, 1998, see entry at **30–106** para. 30–101, n. 27. This decision was not followed in *Re Southern Equities Corp. Ltd., England v. Smith* [2000] 2 B.C.L.C. 21 (C.A.). See entry at para 30–100, n. 13 and text thereto.

NOTE 52. As to *England v. Purves, The Times,* January 29, 1998, see entry at **30–107** para. 30–101, n. 27.

NOTE 54. Add: *Re Southern Equities Corp. Ltd., England v. Smith, supra.*

NOTE 55. As to *England v. Purves, The Times,* January 29, 1998, see entry at para. 30–101, n. 27. Add: *Re Southern Equities Corp. Ltd., England v. Smith, supra.* See entry at para. 30–100, n. 13 and text thereto.

D. *Receivers*

NOTES 68, 69. The provisions of Companies Act 1989 there referred to will **30–111** not now be brought into force, but the Department of Trade and Industry is continuing to review the law relating to the registration of charges: see Lightman and Moss, *The Law of Receivers and Administrators of Companies* (3rd ed. 2000), p. 77.

NOTES 71, 72. See previous entry. **30–112**

NOTES 87–92 and text thereto. The provisions of the Companies Act 1989 **30–116** discussed in this paragraph will not now be brought into force. See entry at para. 30–111, nn. 68, 69.

NOTE 94. In line 7 add: *United States v. Levy* (1999) 45 O.R. (3d) 129. **30–118**

NOTE 95. Add: *United States v. Levy, supra,* at p. 142.

NOTE 5 and text thereto. In *United States v. Levy, supra,* the Ontario court **30–119** was prepared to recognise a receiver appointed by a United States District Court on the basis of the "real and substantial connection" principle enunciated by the Supreme Court of Canada in *Morguard Investments Ltd. v. De Savoye* [1990] 3 S.C.R. 1077, see main work, para. 14–083. The court appeared to be influenced by reciprocity in the sense that had the claims occurred in Canada, they would have given rise to similar relief, *e.g.* the appointment of a receiver to freeze assets: see (1999) 45 O.R. (3d) 129, 143–144.

30–123 NOTE 14. Companies Act 1989, s. 103 will not now be brought into force: see entry at para. 30–111, nn. 68, 69.

E. *The European Union Convention on Insolvency Proceedings*

30–132– The European Union Convention on Insolvency Proceedings which is dis-
139 cussed in these paragraphs has now been replaced by a European Union Regulation on Insolvency Proceedings: see Council Regulation (E.C.) 1346/2000 of May 29, 2000 on Insolvency Proceedings, [2000] O.J. L160/1. The United Kingdom and Ireland have given notice, in accordance with Article 3 of the Protocol on the position of the United Kingdom and Ireland annexed to the Treaty on European Union and the Treaty establishing the European Community, of their wish to take part in the adoption and applica-tion of the Regulation: see Recital, para. (32). Conversely, Denmark, in accordance with Articles 1 and 2 on the position of Denmark annexed to the Treaty on European Union and the Treaty establishing the European Commu-nity, is not participating in the adoption of the Regulation and will not, therefore, be bound by it or subject to its application: Recital, para. (33). The legal basis of the Regulation is said to lie in Articles 61(c), 65 and 67(1) of the E.C. Treaty: see Preamble and Recital, para. (2).

The Regulation, which is binding in its entirety and directly applicable in the Member States in accordance with the Treaty establishing the European Community, will enter into force on May 31, 2002: Art. 47. The provisions it contains are an almost exact replica of the provisions of the Convention discussed in the main work, save, of course, that a Regulation applies in Member States, whereas a Convention applies in Contracting States. Although it was intended that the Convention would be accompanied by an official explanatory report (see main work, para. 30–132, n. 57) no such report will, apparently, accompany the Regulation. The unofficial report (see *ibid.*) on the Convention carried no official status, though it will undoubtedly be helpful to those who have to intepret the Regulation: see also Virgos, *European Commu-nity Convention on Insolvency* (1998). When in force, the provisions of the Regulation will take precedence over any inconsistent provisions in existing national laws. It is worthy of specific note, however, that the Regulation will not apply in the United Kingdom to the extent that it is irreconcilable with the obligations arising in relation to bankruptcy and the winding-up of insolvent companies from any arrangements with Commonwealth countries existing at the time the Regulation enters into force: Art. 44 (3)(b).

References to the European Court under the Regulation will be under Art. 234 of the Treaty establishing the European Community: see main work, para. 11–011.

30–139 After this paragraph insert new material as follows:

F. *UNCITRAL Model Law on Cross-Border Insolvency*

The Insolvency Act 2000 provides[97] that the Secretary of State may, by **30–140** regulations made with the agreement of the Lord Chancellor,[98] make any provision which he considers necessary or expedient for the purpose of implementing "the model law on cross-border insolvency",[99] *i.e.* the model law contained in Annex I of the report of the 30th session of UNCITRAL.[1] Such regulations may, in particular, (a) apply any provision of insolvency law[2] in relation to foreign proceedings,[3] whether begun before or after the regulations enter into force, (b) modify the application of insolvency law, whether in relation to foreign proceedings or otherwise, and (c) amend any provision of section 426 of the Insolvency Act 1986.[4] The relevant provisions of the Act of 2000 entered into force on November 30, 2000.[5] As yet, no relevant regulations have been made. Since the regulations will be critical in determining the effect of the model law on existing United Kingdom law, it is obviously not possible to assess, as yet, the impact of its potential implementation. What follows, therefore, is a brief attempt to identify the principal features of the model law.

Purpose of model law. The purpose of the model law is to provide effective **30–141** mechanisms for dealing with cases of cross-border insolvency with a view to promoting the objectives of: co-operation between the courts and other competent authorities of the enacting State and foreign States involved in such cases; greater legal certainty for trade and investment; fair and efficient administration of cross-border insolvencies that protects the interests of all creditors and other interested parties, including the debtor; protection and maximization of the value of the debtor's assets; and facilitation of the rescue of financially troubled businesses, thereby protecting investment and preserving employment.[6]

Drafting of the model law. The model law is drafted to enable States which **30–142** enact it to insert into the text of any enacted article specific references which will indicate what terms or procedures of national insolvency legislation are to be brought into the particular article. In the particular context of the United

---

[97] Insolvency Act 2000, s. 14(1).

[98] Insolvency Act 2000, s. 14(6)(*a*).

[99] For the text see Fletcher, *Insolvency in Private International Law* (1999), Appendix IV with commentary, Chap. 8; Lightman and Moss, *The Law of Receivers and Administrators of Companies* (3rd ed., 2000), Appendix 5 with commentary at pp. 551–561.

[1] Insolvency Act 2000, s. 14(4). See Report on the work of the 30th session of UNCITRAL, 12–30 May 1997; Official Records of the General Assembly of the United Nations, 52nd session, Supplement No. 17, Annex I, pp. 68–78.

[2] Insolvency law has the same meaning as in Insolvency Act 1986, s. 426(10)(*a*) and (*b*) (as amended by Insolvency Act 2000, Sched. 4, Pt. II): Insolvency Act 2000, s. 14(4).

[3] "Foreign proceedings" has the same meaning as in the model law on cross-border insolvency: Insolvency Act 2000, s. 14(4). The definition in Art. 2(a) of the model law is as follows: "foreign proceeding means a collective judicial or administrative proceeding in a foreign State, including an interim proceeding, pursuant to a law relating to insolvency in which proceeding the assets and affairs of the debtor are subject to control or supervision by a foreign court, for the purpose of reorganisation or liquidation." This definition would appear to exclude administrative receiverships as defined in English law from the scope of the model law; see *post*, para. 30–144.

[4] Insolvency Act 2000, s. 14(2).

[5] Insolvency Act 2000, s. 16(2).

[6] See Preamble to the model law.

Kingdom, such terms and procedures and likely to be contained in the regulations made pursuant to section 14(1) of the Insolvency Act 2000.[7] It should, however, be emphasized that a State is not required to enact all the provisions of the model law and may therefore enact only such provisions as appear to it to be appropriate.

30–143　**Scope of the model law**. The model law does not purport to provide a comprehensive legal regime for the regulation of cross-border insolvency.[8] Thus, for example, the model law contains no rules concerned with the jurisdiction of courts in insolvency matters. Such rules will continue to be found in national law. Similarly, there are no choice of law rules in the model law, so that the relevant choice of law rules to be applied will continue to be found in the national laws of an enacting State. The model law is thus concerned with five principal issues: (i) recognition in the enacting State of foreign insolvency proceedings and the effects of such recognition[9]; (ii) direct rights of access to the courts of the enacting State for foreign representatives[11] and creditors[11]; (iii) the rights of courts and representatives in the enacting State to make requests to courts in foreign jurisdictions for recognition of proceedings commenced in the enacting State and to apply therein for assistance and relief, and for representatives to commence, or participate in, proceedings under the insolvency law of the other State[12]; (iv) co-operation between courts and representatives from different jurisdictions[13]; and (v) co-ordination of concurrent proceedings taking place in two or more jurisdictions.[14] Within these broad headings, more detailed provisions elaborate the particular rules which can be applied, and further elaboration will be contained in any implementing regulations.

30–144　**Insolvency procedures covered**. The key definition of the procedures to which the model law is capable of being applied is found in Article 2(a), referred to above.[15] From this definition it would appear to follow that an administrative receivership under English law would not be covered since that institution is, essentially, not of a collective character. On the other hand, administration under the Insolvency Act 1986 would appear to be included since it is a collective procedure involving the court.[16] It is possible that a creditor's voluntary liquidation is included: for although not initiated by a court order, the procedure is collective in nature and matters may be referred

---

[7] The model law is accompanied by indications, in square brackets, of what it is envisaged should be inserted, as, *e.g.* in Article 1(2): "This Law does not apply to a proceeding concerning [designate any types of entities, such as banks or insurance companies, that are subject to a special insolvency regime in this State and that this State wishes to exclude from this Law]".

[8] Contrast the European Union Regulation on Insolvency Proceedings (*ante*, entry at paras. 30–132—30–139) which purports to provide a comprehensive regime.

[9] Arts. 1(1)(a), 15–24.

[10] Defined in Art. 2(d) as "a person or body, including one appointed on an interim basis, authorized in a foreign proceeding to administer the reorganization or the liquidation of the debtor's assets or affairs or to act as a representative of the foreign proceedings".

[11] Arts. 1(1)(b), (d), 9–14.

[12] Arts. 1(1)(b), 5, 25–27.

[13] Arts. 1(1), 25–27.

[14] Arts. 1(1)(c), 28–32.

[15] See *supra*, n. 3.

[16] A Chapter 11 reorganisation under the United States Bankruptcy Code would also probably qualify.

to the court at any stage. It is clear that a liquidator is included, as will be a provisional liquidator because of the explicit reference in Article 2 (a) to an "interim proceeding". Cases of individual bankruptcy are capable of falling within the definition though whether the model law will apply to individual bankruptcies in England will probably depend on the implementing regulations.

CHAPTER 31

BANKRUPTCY

1. ENGLISH BANKRUPTCIES

A. *Jurisdiction of the English Court*

31R–001 NOTE 2. The European Union Regulation on Insolvency Proceedings (not yet in force), which has replaced the European Union Convention on Insolvency Proceedings, applies to bankruptcy. See *ante*, entry at paras. 30–132—139. The UNCITRAL model law on cross-border insolvency (*ante*, entry at paras. 30–140—144) can apply to bankruptcy but whether it will be so applied will depend on the implementing regulations made pursuant to Insolvency Act 2000, s. 14.

31–003 NOTE 8. Part VIII of Insolvency Act 1986 is amended by Insolvency Act 2000, s. 3 and Sched. 3 but the amendments (which are not yet in force) do not affect the propositions in the text.

31–012 NOTE 36. The provisions of Order 11 are now in CPR, Part 6: see, especially, rr. 6.20–6.30. *Practice Direction* [1988] 1 W.L.R. 461 is replaced by *Practice Direction—Insolvency Proceedings*, para. 10.

B. *Effect of an English bankruptcy as an assignment of property*

31–028 NOTE 87. Insolvency Act 1986, s. 426 (10) is amended by Insolvency Act 2000, Sched. 4, Pt. II, para. 16(3).

31–029 NOTE 90. Add: *Re Southern Equities Corp. Ltd., England v. Smith* [2000] 2 B.C.L.C. 21 (C.A.).

31–030 NOTE 94. In line 3 add: *Re Southern Equities Corp. Ltd., England v. Smith, supra.*

2. FOREIGN BANKRUPTCIES

A. *Effect in England of foreign bankruptcy as an assignment of property*

(2) BANKRUPTCY IN ANY OTHER FOREIGN COUNTRY

31–068 This passage was cited with approval in *Chen Li Hung v Ting Lei Miao* [2000] 1 H.K.L.R.D. 252, 258, (2000) 3 H.K.C.F.A.R. 9, 16.

CHAPTER 32

CONTRACTS. GENERAL RULES

Order 11, r. 1(1)(*d*)(iii) is replaced by CPR, r. 6.20(5)(c).   **32–026**

Text to notes 21 and 22. This passage was approved in *Centrax Ltd. v.*   **32–049**
Citibank NA [1999] 1 All E.R. (Comm.) 557, 562 (C.A.).

It has been held consistently that reinsurance contracts broked in the London   **32–090**
market are impliedly governed by English law: *Gan Insurance Co. Ltd. v. Tai*
Ping Insurance Co. Ltd. [1999] I.L.Pr. 729 (C.A.); *Tiernan v. Magen Insur-*
ance Co. Ltd. [2000] I.L.Pr. 517; *Ace Insurance S.A.-N.V. v. Zurich Insurance*
Co. [2000] 2 Lloyd's Rep. 423.

NOTE 30. The 1996 Accession Convention is now in force: S.I. 2000 No.   **32–012**
1825.

See on conflicting standard terms of contract *Ferguson Shipbuilders Ltd. v.*   **32–101**
Voith Hydro GmbH, 2000 S.L.T. 229; Danneman, in *Lex Mercatoria: Essays*
in Honour of Francis Reynolds (ed. Rose, 2000), p. 199.

NOTE 40. See also *Society of Lloyd's v. Fraser* [1998] C.L.C. 1630, 1652   **32–142**
(C.A.); *Fox v. Henderson Investment Fund Ltd.* [1999] 2 Lloyd's Rep. 303.

See entry at para. 32–026.   **32–156**

NOTE 55. See also *Westacre Investments Inc. v. Jugoimport-SPDR Ltd.* [2000]   **32–325**
Q.B. 288, 304 (C.A.).

CHAPTER 33

PARTICULAR CONTRACTS

1. CERTAIN CONSUMER CONTRACTS

33–039 NOTE 25. The same formula is adopted in The Consumer Protection (Distance Selling) Regulations 2000, Reg. 25(5) (S.I. 2000 No. 2334). These Regulations implement Directive 97/7 of the European Parliament and Council of May 20, 1997 on the protection of consumers in respect of distance contracts, [1997] O.J. L144/19.

2. CONTRACTS OF EMPLOYMENT

33–059 NOTE 84 and text thereto. Employment Rights Act 1996, s. 196 is repealed by Employment Relations Act 1999, s. 32(3). Accordingly, whether rights conferred by the 1996 Act or the 1999 Act extend to employees working outside Great Britain will now depend on the true construction of the relevant legislation. The legislation has been said to apply to employees temporarily working in Great Britain and to employees working outside Great Britain when the employment has a "proper connection with the U.K." See H.C. Deb. 1998–1999, Vol. 336, col. 31. See also, *post,* entry at para. 30–072, nn. 26, 27, 28.

NOTE 85. See previous entry.

33–064 See entry at para. 333–059, n. 84 and text thereto. The principles referred to in this paragraph (and those in para. 33–065) could still be relevant to the determination of the questions of where an employee "habitually" works for the purposes of Art. 6(2)(a) (clause (2)(a) of the Rule) of the Rome Convention.

33–071 NOTE 25. Employment Rights Act 1996, s. 196(5) is repealed by Employment Relations Act 1999, s. 32(3). As to employees employed on board a ship, see Employment Relations Act 1999, s. 32(4).

33–072 NOTES 26, 27, 28. Although the "Posted Workers" Directive ([1997] O.J. L18/1) has not been formally implemented in the United Kingdom by regulations, it has been said that the repeal of Employment Rights Act 1996, s. 196 has facilitated the implementation of the Directive by extending rights which are derived from European Union legislation (and also, presumably, English employment law) to workers who are "temporarily" working in Great Britain: H.C. Deb. 1998–1999, Vol. 336, col. 1. Repeal of section 196 also "means that people who may have worked for some years in the U.K., but who are nevertheless excluded from claiming under the Employment Rights Act 1996 will be able to rely upon the protection of U.K. legislation": *ibid.*

NOTE 35 and text thereto. Employment Rights Act 1996, s. 196(3) is repealed by Employment Relations Act 1999, s. 32(3). The rights conferred by the

Working Time Regulations 1998 may be invoked by employees who are temporarily working in Great Britain.

NOTE 37 and text thereto. Order 11, r. 1(1)(*d*) is replaced by CPR, r. **33–073**
6.20(5).

NOTE 62 and text thereto. Employment Rights Act 1996, s. 196(1) is repealed **33–077**
by Employment Relations Act 1999, s. 32(3). The right to a statement of particulars of employment and minimum periods of notice will apply to employment during any period when the employee is engaged to work wholly or mainly outside Great Britain even if the employee does not ordinarily work in Great Britain and the work outside Great Britain is not for the same employer and even if the law which governs the employee's contract of employment is not the law of England or Scotland.

NOTE 63. Employment Rights Act 1996, s. 196(2),(3), is repealed by Employment Relations Act 1999, s. 32(3).

NOTE 65. Employment Rights Act 1996, s. 196(4) is repealed by Employment Relations Act 1999, s. 32(3). See also Employment Relations Act 1999, ss. 7–9 (leave for family and domestic reasons).

NOTE 66. Employment Rights Act 1996, s. 196(7) is repealed by Employment Relations Act 1999, s. 32(3).

NOTE 67. Employment Rights Act 1996, s. 196(6) is repealed by Employment Relations Act 1999, s. 32(3).

NOTE 76. Add: Trade Union and Labour Relations (Consolidation) Act 1992 **33–081**
is also amended by Employment Relations Act 1999.

NOTE 77. As a consequence of Employment Relations Act 1999, s. 32(1), Trade Union and Labour Relations (Consolidation) Act 1992, s. 285(1) is amended so that the duty to consult employee representatives prior to redundancy dismissals (see 1992 Act, s. 188) is no longer excluded in respect of employees working outside Great Britain.

NOTE 88. Employment Rights Act 1996, s. 196 (3)(*f*) and (3A) are repealed by **33–083**
Employment Relations Act 1999, s. 32(3).

NOTE 89. See Council Regulation 44/2001 (E.C.) of December 22, 2000, Art. 21 ([2001] O.J. L12/1) which will enter into force on March 1, 2002.

NOTE 93. As to the Posted Workers Directive, see *ante*, entry at para. 33–072, **33–084**
nn. 26, 27, 28.

Employment Rights Act 1996, s. 196(3) is repealed by Employment Relations **33–086**
Act 1999, s. 32(3). It would seem, however, that there is a "proper connection with the U.K." sufficient to justify the same result as that reached in Illustration No. 6. See entry at para. 33–059, n. 84.

3. CONTRACTS FOR THE SALE, PLEDGE AND HIRE OF MOVABLES

NOTE 25. On the effect on choice of law clauses where standard terms conflict, **33–091**
see Dannemann in *Lex Mercatoria: Essays in Honour of Francis Reynolds* (ed. Rose, 2000), p. 199, at pp. 206–210.

33–106 NOTE 85. As to Unfair Contract Terms Act 1977, s. 26, see *Ocean Chemical Transport Inc. v. Exnor Craggs Ltd.* [2000] 1 All E.R. (Comm.) 519 (C.A.).

4. CONTRACTS OF INSURANCE AND RE-INSURANCE

33–122 NOTE 53. See also *Society of Lloyd's v. Fraser* [1998] C.L.C. 1630 (C.A.) (contract of membership between Canadian "names" and Lloyd's governed by English law as a result of an express choice).

33–128 NOTE 88. Add: *Youell v. Kara Mara Shipping Co. Ltd.* [2000] 2 Lloyd's Rep. 102.

NOTE 91. *Cf. XL Insurance Ltd. v. Owens Corning* [2000] 2 Lloyd's Rep. 500 where it was held that although the policy of insurance was governed by New York law as a result of an express choice, the arbitration clause contained in the policy was governed by English law since the parties had stipulated for arbitration in London under the provisions of the Arbitration Act 1996.

NOTE 95. In line 3 add: See also *Chase v. Ram Technical Services Ltd.* [2000] 2 Lloyd's Rep. 418.

NOTE 98. And see *XL Insurance Ltd. v. Owens Corning, supra.*

33–137 NOTE 34. See also *Chase v. Ram Technical Services Ltd.* [2000] 2 Lloyd's Rep. 418.

33–199 NOTE 56. *Cf.* Case C–412/98 *Universal General Insurance Co. (UGIC) v. Group Josi Reinsurance Co. S.A.* [2001] Q.B. 68 (re-insurance does not fall within rules applicable to insurance contained in Arts. 7–12A of the 1968 Convention (main work, Rule 28(13), *ante*, entry at para. 11–302) since neither re-insured nor re-insurer could be presumed to be in a weak position compared with the other); *Agnew v. Länsförsäkringsbolagens A.B.* [2000] 2 W.L.R. 497 (H.L.).

33–201 NOTE 63. Add: *Gan Insurance Co. Ltd. v. Tai Ping Insurance Co. Ltd.* [1999] I.L.Pr. 729 (C.A.); *Groupama Navigation et Transports v. Catatumbo C.A. Seguros* [2000] 2 Lloyd's Rep. 350 (C.A.).

33–202 NOTE 64. Add: *Gan Insurance Co. Ltd. v. Tai Ping Insurance Co. Ltd., supra*; *Groupama Navigation et Transports v. Catatumbo C.A. Seguros, supra.*

33–203 NOTE 74 and text thereto. In *Tiernan v. Magen Insurance Co. Ltd.* [2000] I.L. Pr. 517 it was held that where a re-insurance contract was placed on the Lloyd's market in the usual way, the contract was on a Lloyd's form and contained London market clauses, such factors were sufficient to demonstrate with reasonable certainty a choice of English law for the purposes of Article 3(1) of the Rome Convention. In *Gan Insurance Co. Ltd. v. Tai Ping Insurance Co. Ltd., supra*, it was held that although the insurance policy was governed by the law of Taiwan, the re-insurance policy was governed by English law since the contract was made in London between London underwriters and brokers in the conventional way and contained London market clauses, thereby demonstrating with reasonable certainty a choice of English law for the purposes of Article 3(1) of the Rome Convention. See *also Ace*

Insurance S.A.-N.V. v. Zurich Insurance Co. of Europe [2000] 2 Lloyd's Rep. 423.

NOTE 77. Add *Tiernan v. Magen Insurance Co. Ltd., supra*; *Gan Insurance Co. Ltd. v. Tai Ping Insurance Co. Ltd., supra*; *Groupama Navigation et Transports v. Catatumbo C.A. Seguros, supra*; *Ace Insurance S.A.-N.V. v. Zurich Insurance Co. of Europe, supra*.

NOTE 78. The position has been held to be the same under Art. 3 (1) of the Rome Convention: see entry at para. 33–023, n.74 and text thereto.

NOTE 79. Add: *Gan Insurance Co. Ltd. v. Tai Ping Insurance Co. Ltd.,*   **33–204**
supra.

NOTE 81. That such a conclusion can be drawn is supported by *Gan Insurance Co. Ltd. v. Tai Ping Insurance Co. Ltd., supra*, although it was not drawn in this particular case: see entry at para. 33–023, n. 74 and text thereto. And see *Groupama Navigation et Transports v. Catatumbo C.A. Seguros, supra*.

NOTE 82. As was the case in *Gan Insurance Co. Ltd. v. Tai Ping Insurance Co. Ltd., supra*.

NOTE 85. Add: And see *Group Navigation et Transports v. Catatumbo C.A. Seguros, supra*.

NOTES 88 and 89 and text thereto. In *Tiernan v. Magen Insurance Co. Ltd.*   **33–206**
[2000] I.L.Pr. 517, 523, it was said that the characteristic performance of a re-insurance contract was that of the re-insurer.

NOTE 96. *Cf. Tiernan v. Magen Insurance Co. Ltd., supra*.   **33–209**

NOTE 9. See *Gan Insurance Co. Ltd. v. Tai Ping Insurance Co. Ltd., supra*.   **33–211**
See also *Groupama Navigation et Transports v. Catatumbo C.A. Seguros, supra*.

5. CONTRACTS WITH REGARD TO IMMOVABLES

NOTE 52. Add: *Ashurst v. Pollard* [2001] 2 W.L.R. 722 (C.A.).   **33–220**

NOTE 2. The Consumer Protection (Distance Selling) Regulations 2000, regs.   **33–223**
7–20 do not apply to a contract which is a "timeshare agreement" within the meaning of Timeshare Act 1992 and to which that Act applies: Consumer Protection (Distance Selling) Regulations 2000, reg. 6(1).

6. CONTRACTS FOR THE CARRIAGE OF PERSONS OR GOODS GENERALLY

The provisions of Montreal Additional Protocol No. 4, which modernises the   **33–243**
rules on the carriage of cargo by air, were given effect in English law by the Carriage by Air Acts (Implementation of Protocol No. 4 of Montreal, 1975) Order 1999, S.I. 1999 No. 1312. See for parties, S.I. 2000 No. 3061. A new version of the Warsaw Convention, known as the Montreal Convention 1999 was agreed in May 1999; it is not yet in force.

NOTE 52. Carriage by Air Act 1961 (Application of Provisions) Order 1967 is further amended by S.I. 1999 Nos. 1312 and 1737.

7. CONTRACTS OF AFFFREIGHTMENT

33–271   NOTE 75. See also *The Ikariada* [1999] 2 Lloyd's Rep. 365.

33–282   NOTE 10. *Cf. The Ikariada, supra.*

8. CONTRACTS BETWEEN BANKER AND CUSTOMER

33R—289   NOTE 35. Add in line 1 : *Centrax Ltd. v. Citibank N.A.* [1999] 1 All E.R. (Comm.) 557 (C.A.). *Cf. Raiffeisen Zentralbank Osterreich Aktiengesellschaft v. National Bank of Greece S.A.* [1999] 1 Lloyd's Rep. 408, 412.

NOTE 37. Add: *Raiffeisen Zentralbank Osterreich Aktiengesellschaft v. National Bank of Greece S.A., supra.*

33–292   NOTE 51 and text thereto. A banking transaction may be effected under a standard form containing an express choice of law: see *Credit Suisse First Boston (Europe) Ltd. v. M.L.C. (Bermuda) Ltd.* [1999] 1 Lloyd's Rep. 77 (Global Master Repurchase Agreement containing an express choice of English law). See also *Credit Suisse First Boston (Europe) Ltd. v. Seagate Trading Co. Ltd.* [1999] 1 Lloyd's Rep. 784. In penultimate line add: *Centrax Ltd. v. Citibank N.A., supra.*

33–294   NOTE 64. Add: *Centrax Ltd. v. Citibank N.A., supra. Cf. Raiffeissen Zentralbank Osterreich Aktiengesellschaft v. National Bank of Greece S.A., supra,* at p. 412.

33–299   NOTE 99. *Raiffeissen Zentralbank Osterreich Aktiengesellschaft v. National Bank of Greece S.A., supra* (in a "bank to bank" contract under which one bank undertakes to make payment due under a separate loan agreement to another bank and to warrant that there has been no default under the loan agreement, the characteristic performance is that of the bank which makes the payment and provides the warranty).

33–312   NOTE 63. See *Centrax Ltd. v. Citibank N.A.* [1999] 1 All E.R. (Comm.) 557 (C.A.).

NOTE 64 and text thereto. See now Financial Services and Markets Act 2000.

11. INTEREST

33R–371   NOTE 58. Add: Guest in *Lex Mercatoria: Essays in Honour of Francis Reynolds* (ed. Rose, 2000), p. 271.

NOTE 61. As to *Kuwait Oil Tanker Co. SAK v. Al Bader* see [2000] 2 All E.R. (Comm.) 271, 339–344 (C.A.) allowing the appeal in part, but without expressing a concluded view on this point.

33–376   NOTE 76. See also S.I. 1999 No. 1816; S.I. 2000 No. 2225; S.I. 2000 No. 2740.

33–385   NOTES 8–11 and text thereto. In *Kuwait Oil Tanker Co. SAK v. Al Bader* [2000] 2 All E.R. (Comm.) 271, 339–344, the Court of Appeal, in allowing the appeal in part, did not find it necessary to form a concluded view as to whether section 35A of the Supreme Court Act 1981 was procedural (as held by Hobhouse J. in *Midland International Trade Services v. Sudairy, Financial Times*, May 2, 1990 and by Moore-Bick J. in the court below, *The Independent*, January 11, 1999) or substantive as submitted in the main work, para. 33–385. While the Court of Appeal acknowledged (at p. 343) "the force of Hobhouse J.'s reasoning as an analysis of the nature and origins of the English court's general power to award interest," it went on to say (*ibid.*) that "it is also right to observe that the creation of that power creates a right in a claimant to claim interest, which right is recognized and consistently given effect on the basis that it represents compensation to the claimant for having been kept out of money to which he has been held entitled." Additionally, the Court of Appeal expressed no view on the question of whether the right to claim interest by way of damages belonged to the "consequences of breach" for the purposes of Article 10(1)(c) of the Rome Convention since no argument had been heard on this point.

NOTES 14, 15 and text thereto. See previous entry. In *Kuwait Oil Tanker Co.*   **33–386**
SAK v. Al Bader, supra, the Court of Appeal also found it unnecessary to express a view on the question of whether jurisdiction to make an award of compound interest depended on the *lex fori* or on the "double actionability" choice of law rule which was applicable to the tort in that case since, at first instance (*The Independent*, January 11, 1999) Moore-Bick J. had also considered the position under the "double actionability" rule in case he was wrong in his preference for the *lex fori* and had found that a right to compound interest was available on both analyses.

NOTE 48. See entry at para. 33–385, nn. 8–11 and text thereto.   **33–393**

12. CONTRACTS THROUGH AGENTS

A. *Contract of Agency*

NOTE 97. On the use of French law in interpreting the compensation provi-   **33–405**
sions of the Regulations see *Moore v. Piretta Ltd.* [1999] 1 All E.R. 174; see also *Duffen v. Firabo SpA* [2000] 1 Lloyd's Rep 180; *King v. T. Tunnock Ltd.*, 2000 S.L.T. 744.

NOTE 3. On *Ingmar G.B. Ltd. v. Eaton Leonard Technologies Inc.* [1998]   **33–407**
C.L.Y. 115, see now Case C–381/98 *Ingmar G.B. Ltd. v. Eaton Leonard Technologies Inc., The Times*, November 16, 2000.

In Case C–381/98 *Ingmar G.B. Ltd. v. Eaton Leonard Technologies Inc.*,   **33–409—**
supra, the European Court held that Articles 17 and 18 of the Council   **412**
Directive on the co-ordination of the laws of Member States relating to self-employed commercial agents ([1986] O.J. L382/17) implemented in England and Scotland by Commercial Agents (Council Directive) Regulations 1993, regs. 17 and 18, which guarantee certain rights to commercial agents after the termination of an agency contract, must be applied where the commercial agent carries on his activity in a Member State even though the principal is established in a non-Member State and a clause in the contract stipulates that the contract is to be governed by the law of that country. It follows from this

ruling that where a commercial agent carries on activities in England on behalf of a principal established in California under an agency contract governed by Californian law, the 1993 Regulations will apply. The same result should ensue where the agency contract is governed by the law of any non-Member State providing the agent carries on activities in England and the principal is established in any non-Member State.

33–415 Add new Illustration:

8. P, a Californian company, appoints A, an English company, to act as its agent in England. The contract contains a choice of Californian law. Commercial Agents (Council Directive) Regulations 1993, regs. 17 and 18 will govern A's rights after the termination of the contract, irrespective of the choice of Californian law and irrespective of the fact that P is established in a non-Member State: Case C–381/98 *Ingmar G.B. Ltd. v. Eaton Leonard Technologies Inc.*, *The Times*, November 16, 2000.

B. *Relation of Principal and Third Party*

33R–416 NOTE 34. Add in penultimate line: *Azov Shipping Co. v. Baltic Shipping Co.* [1999] 2 Lloyd's Rep. 159, 172; *Grupo Torras S.A. v. Al-Sabah* [1999] C.L.C. 1469, 1505–1506, revd. in part on other grounds, November 2, 2000 (C.A.).

33–421 NOTE 47. Add: *Azov Shipping Co. v. Baltic Shipping Co., supra.*

NOTE 48. Add: *Grupo Torras S.A. v. Al-Sabah, supra.*

33–422 NOTE 54. Whether *e.g.*, a director of a company is authorised to confer actual authority on an agent will depend on Rule 154(2): See *Grupo Torras S.A. v. Al-Sabah, supra.*

33–424 NOTE 58. Add: *Azov Shipping Co. v. Baltic Shipping Co., supra.*

CHAPTER 34

RESTITUTION

NOTE 1. Add Panagopoulos, *Restitution in Private International Law* (2000). **34R–001**

See also *Kuwait Oil Tanker S.A.K. v. Al Bader* [2000] 2 All E.R. (Comm.) **34–004** 271(C.A.), and *Grupo Torras S.A. v. Al Sabah* [2001] C.L.C. 221, (C.A.), discussed in more detail under para. 34–032, *infra*.

See also *Kuwait Oil Tanker S.A.K. v. Al Bader, supra*, and *Grupo Torras S.A.* **34–010** *v. Al Sabah, supra*, which suggest that this category is too wide, and needs to be confined to liability based on receipt, while liability based on wrongful breach of an obligation is treated separately.

NOTE 26. But see *Grupo Torras S.A. v. Al Sabah, supra*, in which it was **34–011** considered more correct to speak of a claim for contribution (which is restitutionary) in respect of (equitable) wrongdoing.

Insert after sixth sentence: But if the claim is not one for the vindication of **34–013** proprietary rights, it will be restitutionary if based on wrongful receipt, though not (and based on a choice of law for wrongdoing) if based on fault: *Kuwait Oil Tanker S.A.K. v. Al Bader, supra*, and *Grupo Torras S.A. v. Al Sabah, supra*, discussed in more detail under para. 34–032, *infra*.

First sentence. Clause (2)(c) was approved in *Kuwait Oil Tanker S.A.K. v. Al* **34–030** *Bader, supra*.

See generally on choice of law for equitable wrongs Yeo (1999) 115 L.Q.R. **34–032** 571.
   The choice of law rule or rules to be applied to cases in which the defendant is alleged to have acted in a manner which, in English law, would be regarded as a breach of fiduciary duty or equitable wrong has been considered by the Court of Appeal in two cases, and this paragraph must now be read in the light of these decisions.
   In *Kuwait Oil Tanker S.A.K. v. Al Bader* [2000] 2 All E.R. (Comm.) 271 (C.A.), the claim against the defendant was primarily formulated in tort, alleging an unlawful conspiracy. But liability was also asserted on the basis that the wrongful acts of the defendant were independently actionable as breaches of the duties of good faith and honesty which had resulted in the unjust enrichment of the defendant. The Court of Appeal held that in such a case, the correct approach was to enquire (1) what was the proper law of the relationship between the defendant and the person for whose benefit the powers and duties are created; (2) what, under that law, are those duties; (3) whether these duties, thus defined, have the general characteristics of being fiduciary according to English standards; and if so, (4) whether it is uncon-scionable for the defendant to retain the assets. As to the first point, the court

applied the law of Kuwait, appearing to do so by reference to Rule 200(2)(c) as being that of the place where the enrichment occurred.

By contrast, a differently constituted court in *Grupo Torras S.A. v. Al Sabah* [2001] C.L.C. 221 (C.A.), agreed that where it was claimed against a defendant that he was liable for his dishonest assistance of another's breach of trust, neither the choice of law rules for restitutionary claims, nor the common law choice of law rules for tort claims (the facts which gave rise to the claim predated the coming into force of the Private International Law (Miscellaneous Provisions) Act 1995, and the court did not say whether the 1995 Act would have applied had the material dates been different) were applicable. It rejected the view that it was appropriate to apply a restitutionary choice of law rule to a claim which was for equitable compensation based on fault; and that there was a single choice of law rule for all claims in which the defendant was alleged to be liable as a constructive trustee. In the result the court, having freed itself from other constraints, applied Spanish law, *semble* as the law where the defendant had carried out those acts from which his liability was alleged to flow, to ascertain that his conduct gave rise to liability; and upon its being shown that it did, the liability which his conduct gave rise to under English law was confirmed and established.

The conclusion to be drawn from these two cases is that a claim which is founded on an allegation of unlawful or knowing receipt or unjust enrichment will fall within the scope of the present Rule. But a claim which is founded on an allegation of wrongdoing for which compensation is due does not do so, even if English domestic law would regard the liability as equitable, and even though an English court would impose the status of constructive trusteeship on the defendant.

34–041   NOTE 24. *Kuwait Oil Tanker S.A.K. v. Al Bader* was affirmed [2000] 2 All E.R. (Comm.) 271 (C.A.); see also *Grupo Torras S.A. v. Al Sabah* [2001] C.L.C. 221 (C.A.), both discussed in more detail under para. 34–032, *supra*.

CHAPTER 35

TORTS

1. THE LAW APPLICABLE TO ISSUES IN TORT

NOTE 25. Add: Symeonides (1999) 47 Am. J. Comp. L. 322; (2000) 48 Am.   **35–004**
J. Comp. L. 143.

NOTE 33. *Pearce v. Ove Arup Partnership Ltd.* is now reported at [2000] Ch.   **35–005**
403 (C.A.). *Kuwait Oil Tanker Co. SAK v. Al Bader* is now reported at [2000]
2 All E.R. (Comm.) 271 (C.A.) affirming in part and reversing in part on other
grounds the decision of Moore-Bick J., *The Independent*, January 11, 1999.

NOTE 34. See now *Lubbe v. Cape plc* [2000] 1 W.L.R. 1545 (H.L.) affirming,
without reference to the point, [1999] I.L.Pr. 113 (C.A.), and reversing the
second Court of Appeal decision in this case reported at [2000] 1 Lloyd's Rep.
139, 155. As to *Kuwait Oil Tanker Co. SAK v. Al Bader*, see previous
entry.

NOTE 37. In line 6 add: *George v. Gubernowicz* (1999) 44 O.R. (3d) 247;
Buchan v. Non-Marine Underwriters, Members of Lloyd's of London, England
(1999) 44 O.R. (3d) 685; *Wong v. Wei* [1999] 10 W.W.R. 296 (B.C.)

NOTE 38 and text thereto. In *John Pfeiffer Pty. Ltd. v. Rogerson* (2000) 172
A.L.R. 625 the High Court of Australia discarded the rule of double actionability in respect of torts committed in Australia which possessed an interstate
element. It was held that the common law of Australia should now be
developed (Gleeson C.J., Gaudron, McHugh, Gummow and Hayne JJ.) or
re-expressed (Kirby J.) so that the *lex loci delicti* is the governing law.
Application of this law by courts exercising federal jurisdiction and non-
federal jurisdiction reflected the fact that the tort is committed within a
federation and, more particularly, recognized and gave effect to the statutes of
the legislatures of the States and Territories, as required by section 118 (the
"full faith and credit clause") of the Australian Constitution. The High Court
expressly refused to follow *Phillips v. Eyre* (1870) L.R. 6 Q.B.1, *Koop v. Bebb*
(1951) 84 C.L.R. 629, *Anderson v. Eric Anderson Radio & TV Pty. Ltd.* (1965)
114 C.L.R. 20, *McKain v. R.W. Miller & Co. (South Australia) Pty. Ltd.* (1991)
104 A.L.R. 257 and *Stevens v. Head* (1993) 176 C.L.R. 463 and regarded
Breavington v. Godleman (1988) 169 C.L.R. 41 as inconclusive since the
constitutional dimension of the problem was not considered in that case. It
was further held that, in an interstate context, there was no room for an
exception to the application of the *lex loci delicti*. The court expressed no
considered view on the relevant choice of law rules to be applied in cases
where the foreign element in the case was supplied by a connection with a
foreign (*i.e.* non-Australian) jurisdiction (see Gleeson C.J., at p. 647, Kirby J.
at p. 655). However, in *Zhang v. Régie Nationale des Usines Renault S.A.*,
N.S.W.C.A. July 27, 2000 (not yet reported), the New South Wales Court of
Appeal held that despite *Pfeiffer*, the double actionability rule continued to

apply in international cases. For further comment on the *Pfeiffer* case, see *post*, entry at paras. 35–053—35–055.

35–006 NOTE 41. *Pearce v. Ove Arup Partnership Ltd.* is now reported at [2000] Ch. 403 (C.A.). For *Lubbe v. Cape plc* [2000] 1 W.L.R. 1545 (H.L.) see entry at para. 35–005, n. 33. Add: *Kuwait Oil Tanker Co. SAK v. Al Bader* [2000] 2 All E.R. (Comm.) 271 (C.A.).

35–008 NOTE 54. As to *Lubbe v. Cape plc*, see previous entry.

35–010 NOTE 58. *Pearce v. Ove Arup Partnership Ltd.* is now reported at [2000] Ch. 403 (C.A.).

35–013 NOTE 78. See entry at para. 35–010, n. 58.

35–014 NOTE 82. See *Kuwait Oil Tanker Co. SAK v. Al Bader* [2000] 2 All E.R. (Comm.) 271, 330 (C.A.).

35–021 NOTE 1. See *Edmunds v. Simmonds, The Times*, November 21, 2000. And see *post*, entry at para. 35–093.

35–022 NOTE 6. See entry at para. 35–010, n. 58.

35–028 NOTE 16. See entry at para. 35–010, n. 58.

35–029 NOTE 26. See entry at para. 35–010, n. 58.

35–030 NOTES 31, 32, 35. See entry at para. 35–010, n. 58.

35–033 NOTE 39. Add: See also *John Pfeiffer Pty. Ltd. v. Rogerson* (2000) 172 A.L.R. 625, 649.

NOTE 43. See also *John Pfeiffer Pty. Ltd. v. Rogerson, supra*, at p. 665.

NOTE 45. Add: *Buchan v. Non-Marine Underwriters, Members of Lloyd's of London, England* (1999) 44 O.R. (3d) 247.

35–033 NOTE 47. *Koop v. Bebb* was not followed by the High Court of Australia in *John Pfeiffer Pty. Ltd. v. Rogerson* (2000) 172 A.L.R. 625: see *ante*, entry at para. 35–006, n. 38.

35–034 NOTE 49. See also *Buchan v. Non-Marine Underwriters, Members of Lloyd's of London, England* (1999) 44 O.R. (3d) 685. As to *Koop v. Bebb*, see previous entry.

35–042 NOTES 96, 98. The point did not arise in *John Pfeiffer Pty. Ltd. v. Rogerson, supra*, and was expressly reserved by Kirby J., at p. 665.

35–049 NOTE 18. The point did not arise in *John Pfeiffer Pty. Ltd. v. Rogerson, supra*, and was expressly reserved by Kirby J., at p. 665.

35–049 NOTE 24 and text thereto. In *Edmunds v. Simmonds, The Times*, November 21, 2000, it was stated that Part III of the Private International Law (Miscellaneous Provisions) Act 1995 had not abrogated the distinction between substance and procedure, and that section 14(3)(*b*) of the Act expressly reserved questions of procedure for determination in accordance with the law of the forum.

NOTE 27. In *John Pfeiffer Pty. Ltd. v. Rogerson, supra*, it was stated (in the context of interstate cases arising within Australia) that only the rules regulating the mode or conduct of court proceedings were procedural.

NOTE 28. *Cf. John Pfeiffer Pty. Ltd. v. Rogerson, supra.*   **35–051**

NOTES 35, 36 and text thereto. In *Edmunds v. Simmonds, supra*, it appears to   **35–053** have been held that questions relating to the quantification or assessment of damages were matters of procedure to be determined by the law of the forum, and that the 1995 Act did not affect this position. *Cf. John Pfeiffer Pty. Ltd. v. Rogerson* (2000) 172 A.L.R. 625 where it was held (in the context of torts committed within Australia) that all matters affecting the existence, extent or enforceability of the rights and duties of the parties to an action, including all questions of the type or amount or damages recoverable were matters of substance governed (in the view of Australian law) by the law of the place of the tort. In *Wong v. Wei* [1999] 10 W.W.R. 296 (B.C.) it was held that the issue of quantification of damages was procedural, though the court appears to have contemplated that if it was not, then the application of the higher measure of damages under the *lex loci delicti*, the law of California, would be denied since both parties were Canadian citizens, ordinarily resident in British Columbia.

NOTES 43, 44. Add: *Edmunds v. Simmonds, supra*; *Wong v. Wei, supra*; *John*   **35–055** *Pfeiffer Pty. Ltd. v. Rogerson, supra* (heads of damage a matter of substance to be determined by the law applicable to the tort).

NOTE 48. *Stevens v. Head* (1993) 176 C.L.R. 433 was not followed by the High Court of Australia in *John Pfeiffer Pty. Ltd. v. Rogerson, supra*. In the latter case it was stated that the existence and extent of financial ceilings on recoverable damages were questions of substantive law. See also *Wong v. Wei* (1999) 10 W.W.R. 296 (B.C.).

NOTE 51 and text thereto. The point was not adverted to in *John Pfeiffer Pty.*   **35–056** *Ltd. v. Rogerson, supra*, and was expressly reserved by Kirby J., at p. 665.
    Add: See Takahashi, *Claims for Contribution and Reimbursement in an International Context* (2000), Chap. 3.

NOTE 63. See also *Kuwait Oil Tanker Co. SAK v. Al Bader* [2000] 2 All E.R.   **35–060** (Comm.) 271, 335–336 (C.A.).

NOTES 77, 78. See also *Grupo Torras S.A. v. Al-Sabah* [2001] C.L.C. 221   **35–064** (C.A.); *Kuwait Oil Tanker Co. SAK v. Al Bader, supra*; entry at para. 34–032, *ante*.

2. DETERMINATION OF THE APPLICABLE LAW

A. *The General Rule*

NOTE 61 and text thereto. In *Edmunds v. Simmonds, The Times*, November 21,   **35–080** 2000, a case arising out of a motor accident in Spain, the *lex loci delicti*,

Spanish law, was displaced in favour of English law, pursuant to section 12 of the 1995 Act (Rule 203). See *post*, entry at para. 30–093.

35–082   NOTE 66. For *Lubbe v. Cape plc* [2000] 1 W.L.R. 1545 (H.L.) see entry at para. 35–005, n. 33.

35–085   NOTE 76. See previous entry.

35–086   NOTE 80. Add: *Grupo Torras S.A. v. Al-Sabah* [1999] C.L.C. 1469, 1653–1657, revd. in part on other grounds [2001] C.L.C. 221, (C.A.); *Kuwait Oil Tanker Co. SAK v. Al Bader* [2000] 2 All E.R. (Comm.) 271, 332–333 (C.A.). (conspiracy).

35–088   NOTE 85. *Pearce v. Ove Arup Partnership Ltd.* is now reported at [2000] Ch. 403 (C.A.).

B. *Rule of Displacement*

35R–091   NOTE 97. Add: *Edmunds v. Simmonds, The Times*, November 21, 2000.

NOTE 98. Add: *Edmunds v. Simmonds, supra.*

35–092   NOTE 1. *Pearce v. Ove Arup Partnership Ltd.* is now reported at [2000] Ch. 403 (C.A.). *For Lubbe v. Cape plc.* [2000] 1 W.L.R. 1545 (H.L.) see entry at para. 35–005, n. 33.

Add: *Grupo Torras S.A. v. Al-Sabah* [2001] C.L.C. 221 (C.A.); *Kuwait Oil Tanker Co. SAK v. Al Bader* [2000] 2 All E.R. (Comm.) 271 (C.A.).

NOTE 2. In line 8 add. See also *Wong v. Wei* [1999] 10 W.W.R. 296 (B.C.) applying the *lex fori* despite the fact that the tort was committed in California.

Add at end: *George v. Gubernowicz* (1999) 44 O.R. (3d) 685. In *John Pfeiffer Pty. Ltd. v. Rogerson* (2000) 172 A.L.R. 625 where the High Court of Australia discarded the rule of double actionability in favour of a choice of law rule requiring reference to the *lex loci delicti* (*ante*, entry at para. 35–006, n. 38), it was stated that no exception should exist to the application of this law.

35–093   NOTE 3 and text thereto. In *Edmunds v. Simmonds, The Times*, November 21, 2000, the claimant suffered personal injuries while travelling as a passenger in a hire-car driven by the defendant in Spain. The car had been hired in Spain by the parties who were on holiday in that country. The accident was caused by the defendant negligently losing control of the car which, in consequence, collided with a Spanish lorry. The car was insured by a Spanish insurer. It appeared that although there was no relevant difference between Spanish law and English law on the issue of liability, the method of assessing the quantum of damages in each system was wholly different and likely to result in a much lower award to the claimant if Spanish law were applied on this issue. Garland J. held that the quantification of damages was to be determined by reference to English law. This conclusion could be reached pursuant to section 14(3)(*b*) of the 1995 Act since that sub-section expressly referred questions of procedure to the *lex fori* and the question of quantification of damages was to be classified as procedural: see main work, paras. 35–052—055; *ante*, entry at para 35–053, nn. 35, 36 and text thereto). However, Garland J. also considered that if Spanish law was applicable to the substantive issue of heads of damage, pursuant to section 11(1) of the 1995 Act, there was an overwhelming case for the displacement of that law, in favour of English law, pursuant to section 12 of the 1995 Act. Since the accident had arisen out of the defendant's loss of control of the car, the involvement of the Spanish lorry was irrelevant and, in consequence, the only Spanish element present in the case was the involvement of the Spanish insurer. But this factor was not of overwhelming weight, as insurers of hire-cars in tourist areas or those who provide fly-drive services must contemplate that the majority of hirers would be foreign and accidents involving them might result in damages being quantified according to a different system of law. In making the comparison required by section 12, the factors connecting the tort to England were overwhelming and it was substantially more appropriate that damages were assessed according to English law. This was because (*cf. Boys v. Chaplin* [1971] A.C. 356) heads of damage were strongly linked to the country where the claimant normally resided, a link rendered stronger when the defendant resided in the same country and no policy or interest of Spain was infringed by one English resident being required to compensate another English resident according to the heads of damage available in English law.

NOTES 5–7 and text thereto. In *Edmunds v. Simmonds, supra*, while Spanish law seems to have been regarded as determinative of liability, the issue of heads of damage was held to be governed by English law: see previous entry.   **35–095**

NOTE 8. For *Lubbe v. Cape plc* [2000] 1 W.L.R. 1545 (H.L.) see entry at para. 35–005, n. 33. *Pearce v. Ove Arup Partnership Ltd.* is now reported at [2000] Ch. 403 (C.A.).

NOTES 16–22 and text thereto. See the discussion in *Edmunds v. Simmonds, The Times*, November 21, 2000, *ante*, entry at para. 35–093, n. 3 and text thereto.   **35–099**

NOTE 25. See previous entry.   **35–100**

NOTE 26 and text thereto. See the discussion *in Edmunds v. Simmonds, supra*, entry at para. 35–093, n. 3 and text thereto.   **35–101**

NOTE 28. As to *Lubbe v. Cape plc*, see entry at para. 35–005, n. 33.

NOTES 29–31. See the discussion in *Edmunds v. Simmonds, supra, ante*, entry at para. 35–093, n. 3 and text thereto.   **35–102**

NOTES 32, 33. The correctness of these submissions appears to be supported by *Edmunds v. Simmonds, supra, ante*, entry at para. 35–093, n. 3 and text thereto.   **35–103**

NOTES 34, 35. See previous entry.   **35–104**

NOTE 40. See *Codd v. Thomson Tour Operations Ltd., The Times*, October 20, 2000 (C.A.) (although English law applied in respect of the establishment   **35–105** of negligence, Spanish rather than English safety standards were the appropriate standards to apply in respect of a hotel in Majorca).

35–107 Add new Illustration:

7. A, an English resident, is injured in a motor accident in Spain caused by the negligence of X, also an English resident, who lost control of the car in which A was a passenger and collided with a Spanish lorry. A and X had hired the car in Spain where they were on holiday. The car was insured by Spanish insurers.

There is no difference between Spanish law and English law on the issue of the defendant's liability but, under Spanish law, A would be likely to receive an award of damages substantially less than would be available under English law. Spanish law determines the question of liability.[58a] Since the question of quantification of damages is procedural, English law applies to this question.[58b] With regard to heads of damages, a question of substance, although Spanish law applies as a general rule,[58c] in the light of a comparison between the significance of the factors which connect the tort with Spain and those that connect the tort with England,[58d] it is substantially more appropriate for this issue to be determined by English law.[58e]

3. PUBLIC POLICY AND RELATED QUESTIONS

35–112 NOTE 63. The Human Rights Act 1998 entered into force on October 2, 2000.

NOTE 64. The European Court of Justice has referred to decisions of the European Convention on Human Rights in the context of public policy as contained in Article 27(1) of the 1968 Convention: see Case C–7/98 *Krombach v. Bamberski* [2000] E.C.R. I–1935; Case C–38/98 *Régie Nationale des Usines Renault S.A. v. Maxicar SpA*, May 11, 2000.

35–113 NOTE 68. See also *Wong v. Wei* (1999) 10 W.W.R. 296 (B.C.).

4. LAW APPLICABLE TO DEFAMATION AND RELATED CLAIMS

35–125 NOTE 11. See *Kyu Ho Hum* (2000) 49 I.C.L.Q. 131.

NOTE 19. *Pearce v. Ove Arup Partnership Ltd.* is now reported at [2000] Ch. 403 (C.A.). *Kuwait Oil Tanker Co. SAK v. Al Bader* [2000] 2 All E.R. (Comm.) 271 (C.A.) affirmed in part and reversed in part on other grounds the decision of Moore-Bick J., *The Independent*, January 11, 1999. For *Lubbe v. Cape plc* [2000] 1 W.L.R. 1545 (H.L.) see entry at para. 35–005, n. 33.

35–126 NOTE 21 and text thereto. Order 11, r. 1(1)(*f*) is replaced by CPR, r. 6.20 (8).

35–129 NOTE 35. As to *Lubbe v. Cape plc*, see *ante*, entry at para. 35–005, n. 33. Add at end: See also *Kuwait Oil Tanker Co. SAK v. Al Bader* [2000] 2 All E.R. (Comm.) 271 (C.A.).

[58a] Private International Law (Miscellaneous Provisions) Act 1995, s.11(1); *Edmunds v. Simmonds, The Times*, November 21, 2000.
[58b] 1995 Act, s.14(3)(b); *Edmunds v. Simmonds, supra*.
[58c] 1995 Act, s.11(1).
[58d] 1995 Act, s.12.
[58e] 1995 Act, s.12; *Edmunds v. Simmonds, supra*.

NOTE 43. As to *Pearce v. Ove Arup Partnership Ltd.* and *Lubbe v.Cape plc*, **35–131**
see entry at para. 35–125, n. 19. Add at end: *Grupo Torras S.A. v. Al-Sabah*
[2001] C.L.C. 221 (C.A.).

NOTE 48. See entry at para. 35–125, n. 19. **35–132**

NOTES 74–77 and text thereto. The views expressed in the main work were **35–139**
discussed in *Kuwait Oil Tanker Co. SAK v. Al Bader* [2000] 2 All E.R.
(Comm.) 271, 335–336 (C.A.) and it was said that whether or not the claimant
incorporates in his pleading an averment that the matters relied on are civilly
actionable under the *lex loci delicti*, the burden in practice lies upon the
defendant to plead and prove that his conduct was not actionable under the *lex
loci delicti*. The debate between the two views referred to in the main work
was thus a "somewhat arid one" (at p. 336) which was likely to give rise to
controversy only at the interlocutory stages of an action where the court is
concerned to consider and give directions in relation to any issue of foreign
law arising on the face of the pleadings and as to the form and extent of any
expert evidence sought to be adduced by the parties. The court expressed the
view that questions of where the burden lies and its practical consequences for
the progress of the action were best dealt with on a case by case basis than by
the application of an inflexible rule.

NOTE 86. As to *McKain v. R.W. Miller & Co. (South Australia.) Pty. Ltd.* **35–146**
(1991) 104 A.L.R. 257, see now *John Pfeiffer Pty. Ltd. v. Rogerson* (2000)
172 A.L.R. 625, *ante*, entry at para. 35–006, n. 38 and text thereto.

CHAPTER 36

FOREIGN CURRENCY OBLIGATIONS

36–008 NOTES 26 and 27. As from January 1, 2001 the euro is the currency of Greece. See Council Decision (E.C.) 427/00, which abrogates the derogation in favour of Greece laid down in recital 4 of Council Decision (E.C.) No. 317/98.

36–064 NOTE 65. The range of contracts to which the 1998 Act applies has been extended by S.I. 1999 No. 1816, S.I. 2000 No. 2225 and S.I. 2000 No. 2740.